Arthur Hyde Lay

Chinese Characters for the Use of Students of the Japanese

Language

Arthur Hyde Lay

Chinese Characters for the Use of Students of the Japanese Language

ISBN/EAN: 9783337003494

Printed in Europe, USA, Canada, Australia, Japan

Cover: Foto ©Paul-Georg Meister /pixelio.de

More available books at **www.hansebooks.com**

CHINESE CHARACTERS

FOR THE

USE OF STUDENTS OF THE JAPANESE LANGUAGE.

ARTHUR HYDE LAY

H. B. M.'s CONSULAR SERVICE.

PRINTED BY
The Ekisei-kwan.
TOKIO:
1897.

PREFACE TO THE SECOND EDITION.

The first Edition has been carefully revised.

In the preparation of this book the object aimed at has been to put into the hands of Students a selected list of about 4,000 of the Chinese Characters which are most useful in studying the Japanese language. Anyone mastering the characters given will be able to read the columns of the Japanese press with ease.

The following method of using the book has been suggested by someone who asserts that it has proved of advantage to a number of people. The student adopting it will, at the end of two years, have no difficulty in writing to dictation, or giving the meanings of, all the characters contained in this work.

Begin with the first character, copy it out, using a Japanese pen, and after writing it several times, cover the character in the book with a slip of paper, and then rewrite it from memory, looking only at the Chinese sounds and English and Japanese meanings. Again, copy out the second character, forming it from memory in the same way, and afterwards go back to the first. Continue to repeat all the characters until the first page has been learnt. Then reverse the order, and learning the meanings and Japanese readings of the characters, endeavour to repeat them, looking only at the characters. Next day commit the second page to memory in a similar fashion, and subsequently return to the first page, merely tracing the characters this time with the finger. Continue to go over daily all that has previously been done, till ten pages have been studied, and after that omit one page each day, repeating however all the pages omitted at least once a week until the book is finished.

Of course for the practical use of the characters the student must read some standard books, such as the Government readers, and the newspapers.

I have to thank R. J. Kirby Esq. of Tokio for his kindness in revising the proof sheets.

ARTHUR HYDE LAY.

H. B. M. LEGATION,
TOKIO.
December 1897.

RADICALS. (1)

1. 一	2. 丨	3. 丶	4. 丿	5. 乙
ITSU, ICHI.	KON.	CHU.	HETSU.	ITSU, OTSU.
Hitotsu.	Tate, susumu, shirizoku.	Shirushi.	Hidari e modoru.	Kinoto.
One.	A connecting line perpendicularly, to pass through.	A mark, point.	A stroke to the left.	A calendar sign.
Page 9.	Page 9.	Page 9.	Page 10.	Page 10.
6. 亅	7. 二	8. 亠	9. 人	10. 儿
KETSU.	JI, NI.	TŌ.	JIN, NIN.	JIN.
Kagi.	Futatsu.	Futa.	Hito.	Hito.
A hook, to mark off.	Two.	A cover. (This radical is always placed on the top).	Man. (亻 Nim-ben.)	Man.
Page 10.	Page 10.	Page 11.	Page 11.	Page 17.
11. 入	12. 八	13. 冂	14. 冖	15. 冫
JŪ, NIŪ.	HATSU, HACHI.	KEI.	BEKI. (Beki-gashira.) Ōu.	HIŌ. (Nisui.) Kōri.
Iru.	Yatsu.	Maki.		
To enter.	Eight.	A border, limit.	To cover.	Ice.
Page 18.	Page 18.	Page 18.	Page 19.	Page 19.
16. 几	17. 凵	18. 刀	19. 力	20. 勹
KI.	KAN.	TŌ.	RIKI, RIOKU.	HŌ.
Tsukue.	Kuchiharu.	Katana.	Chikara.	Tsutsumu.
A low table, bench, desk.	A receptacle, to open the mouth.	A sword. (刂 Ritto.)	Strength.	To wrap up, envelope.
Page 20.	Page 20.	Page 20.	Page 22.	Page 23.
21. 匕	22. 匚	23. 匸	24. 十	25. 卜
HI.	HŌ.	KEI. (Kakushi-gamae.) Kakusu, kakomi.	JŪ, SHŪ. Tō.	BOKU. Uranau.
Saji.	Hako.			
A spoon.	A box, receptacle.	A case or coffer for storing, to conceal.	Ten.	To divine.
Page 23.	Page 23.	Page 24.	Page 24.	Page 24.
26. 卩	27. 厂	28. 厶	29. 又	30. 口
SETSU.	GAN. (Gandare.) Iwao.	SHI, BŌ. Watakushi, katamashii.	YŪ. Mata.	KŌ, KU. Kuchi.
Warifu.				
A seal.	A cliff.	Private, selfish, depraved.	Again.	The mouth, entrance.
Page 25.	Page 25.	Page 25.	Page 25.	Page 26.

31. 口	32. 土	33. 士	34. 夂	35. 夊
I.	To, DO.	SHI.	SHI.	SUI.
Meguri, kakomi.	Tsuchi.	Samurai, tsukasa.	Okureru.	Yasushi.
An enclosure.	Earth.	A samurai, officer.	To follow.	To walk slowly.
Page 31.	Page 31.	Page 34.	Page 34.	Page 34.
36. 夕	37. 大	38. 女	39. 子	40. 宀
SEKI.	DAI, TAI.	JŌ, NIŪ.	SHI.	BEN, MEN. (U-kammuri.)
Yūbe.	Ōi naru.	Onna.	Ko.	Kasanefuku.
Evening.	Great.	A woman, female, daughter.	A child, boy, son.	A roof, cover.
Page 34.	Page 35.	Page 36.	Page 38.	Page 39.
41. 寸	42. 小	43. 尢	44. 尸	45. 屮
SUN.	SHŌ.	Ō.	SHI.	TETSU.
Hakaru.	Chiisai, sukoshi.	Kagamaru.	Shikabane.	Kusa hae izuru.
An inch, to measure.	Small, little.	Bent, crooked. (兌, 尤.)	A corpse.	A plant sprouting.
Page 41.	Page 41.	Page 41.	Page 41.	Page 42.
46. 山	47. 巛	48. 工	49. 己	50. 巾
SAN, SEN.	SEN.	KŌ, KU.	KI, KO.	KIN. (Kim-pen.)
Yama.	Kawa, nagareru.	Takumi.	Onore.	Tenugui.
A hill, mountain.	A river, to flow.	Art, work.	Self.	A napkin, handkerchief.
Page 42.	Page 44.	Page 44.	Page 44.	Page 44.
51. 干	52. 幺	53. 广	54. 廴	55. 廾
KAN.	YŌ.	GEN, KAN. (Madare.)	IN. (In-niu.)	KIŌ.
Tate, okasu.	Wakai.	Iwaya.	Hiku.	Awaseru.
A shield, to oppose.	Young.	A shelter, covering.	To draw.	To join (hands).
Page 45.	Page 46.	Page 46.	Page 47.	Page 47.
56. 弋	57. 弓	58. 彐	59. 彡	60. 彳
YOKU.	KIŪ.	KEI.	SAN, SEN. (Sanzukuri.)	TEKI. (Giō-nimben.)
Igurumi.	Yumi.	I-no kashira.	Ke no kazari.	Tatazumu.
An arrow with cord attached.	A bow.	A pig's head, hog with short upturned.	Ornaments for the hair, feathers.	To stop.
Page 47.	Page 47.	Page 48.	Page 48.	Page 48.

61. 心 **SHIN.** *Kokoro.* The heart, mind. († *Risshin-ben.*) Page 49.	62. 戈 **KWA.** *Hoko.* A spear. Page 55.	63. 戸 **KO.** *To.* A door. Page 55.	64. 手 **SHU.** *Te.* The hand. (扌 *Te-hen.*) Page 56.	65. 支 **SHI.** *Eda.* A branch. Page 62.	
66. 攴 **HAKU.** *Utsu.* To strike. Page 62.	67. 文 **BUN, MON.** *Fumi.* A letter, pattern, crest. Page 63.	68. 斗 **TŌ, TO.** *Masu.* A measure. Page 63.	69. 斤 **KIN.** *Ono.* An axe. Page 63.	70. 方 **HŌ.** *Kata.* Side, square. Page 63.	
71. 无 **BU, MU.** *Nashi.* Not, without. Page 64.	72. 日 **JITSU, NICHI, NITSU.** (*Hi-hen.*) *Hi.* The sun, day. Page 64.	73. 曰 **ETSU.** *Iu.* To speak. Page 66.	74. 月 **GETSU, GWATSU.** (*Tsuki-hen.*) *Tsuki.* Moon. Page 66.	75. 木 **BOKU, MOKU.** (*Ki-hen.*) *Ki.* A tree, wood. Page 67.	
76. 欠 **KEN, KETSU.** (*Ken-tsukuri.*) *Akubi.* To yawn. Page 72.	77. 止 **SHI.** *Todomaru.* To stop. Page 73.	78. 歹 **KATSU.** *Sarebone.* Dry bones. Page 73.	79. 殳 **SHU.** (*Ru-mata.*) *Hoko.* A spear. Page 73.	80. 毋 **BU, MU, BŌ.** *Nashi, nakare.* Not, do not. Page 74.	
81. 比 **HI.** *Tagui, narabu.* Sort, kind, to compare. Page 74.	82. 毛 **MŌ.** *Ke.* Hair, fur, feathers. Page 74.	83. 氏 **SHI.** *Uji.* Surname. Page 74.	84. 气 **KI, KITSU.** *Iki.* Breath, vapour. Page 74.	85. 水 **SUI.** *Mizu.* Water. (氵 *San-zui.*) Page 75.	
86. 火 **KWA.** *Hi.* Fire. (灬 *Rengwa.*) Page 81.	87. 爪 **SŌ.** *Tsume.* Nails, claws. (爫 *Tsume-kammuri.*) Page 83.	88. 父 **FU, HO.** *Chichi.* Father. Page 83.	89. 爻 **KŌ.** *Majiwaru.* To mix. Page 83.	90. 爿 **HAN, SHŌ.** (*Shō-hen.*) *Katami.* One side, one of two. Page 83.	

91. 片	92. 牙	93. 牛	94. 犬	95. 玄
HEN, HAN.	GA, GE.	GIŪ.	KEN.	GEN.
Katagata.	Kiba.	Ushi.	Inu.	Kuroi.
One side.	A tooth.	Cattle. (牛 Ushi-hen.)	Dog. (犭 Kemono-hen.)	Black, dark.
Page 83.	Page 83.	Page 84.	Page 84.	Page 85.
96. 玉	97. 瓜	98. 瓦	99. 甘	100. 生
GIOKU.	KWA.	GWA.	KAN.	SEI, SHŌ.
Tama.	Uri.	Kawara.	Amai.	Umu.
A gem, precious stone. (王 Tama-hen.)	A melon.	A tile.	Sweet.	To produce, bear, live.
Page 86.	Page 87.	Page 87.	Page 87.	Page 87.
101. 用	102. 田	103. 疋	104. 疒	105. 癶
YŌ.	DEN.	SHO.	TAKU. (Yamai-dare.) Yamai.	HATSU.
Mochiiru.	Ta.	Ashi.		Yuku.
To use.	A field.	A foot.	A disease.	To go.
Page 87.	Page 87.	Page 88.	Page 88.	Page 90.
106. 白	107. 皮	108. 皿	109. 目	110. 矛
HAKU.	HI. (Kawa-hen.)	BEI, MIŌ.	MOKU.	MŌ, BŌ, MU.
Shiroi.	Kawa.	Sara.	Me.	Hoko.
White.	Skin, leather, bark.	A dish.	The eye. (目 Me-hen.)	A spear.
Page 90.	Page 91.	Page 91.	Page 91.	Page 92.
111. 矢	112. 石	113. 示	114. 肉	115. 禾
SHI.	SEKI.	SHI. (Shimesu-hen.) Shimesu. (衤)	JŪ.	KWA. (Nogi-hen.)
Ya.	Ishi.		Ashiato.	Ine, nae, awa.
An arrow, dart.	A stone.	To show, publish.	A footprint.	Grain, rice.
Page 93.	Page 93.	Page 94.	Page 95.	Page 95.
116. 穴	117. 立	118. 竹	119. 米	120. 糸
KETSU. (Ana-kammuri.)	RITSU, RIŪ.	CHIKU. (Take-kammuri.)	BEI, MAI. (Kome-hen.)	SHI.
Ana.	Tatsu.	Take.	Kome, yone.	Ito.
A cave, hole.	To stand.	Bamboo.	Rice.	Fine thread.
Page 97.	Page 97.	Page 98.	Page 100.	Page 101.

121. 缶	122. 网	123. 羊	124. 羽	125. 老
Fu, Fū.	Mō, Bō.	Yō.	U.	Rō.
Hodogi.	Ami.	Hitsuji.	Hane.	Toshiyori.
An earthen vessel.	A net.	A sheep, goat.	Feathers, wings.	Old.
Page 104.	Page 105.	Page 105.	Page 106.	Page 106.
126. 而	127. 耒	128. 耳	129. 聿	130. 肉
Ji, Ni.	Rai.	Ji, Ni.	Itsu.	Niku.
Shikōshite, nanji.	Suki.	Mimi, nomi.	Fude.	Shishi.
Yet, still, you.	A plough.	The ear, only, a final particle.	A pen, pencil.	Flesh, meat. (肉 Niku-zuki.)
Page 106.	Page 106.	Page 106.	Page 108.	Page 108.
131. 臣	132. 自	133. 至	134. 臼	135. 舌
Shin.	Ji.	Shi.	Kiū.	Zetsu.
Kerai.	Yori, mizukara.	Itaru.	Usu.	Shita.
A retainer, minister, officer, subject.	From, one's self.	A reach.	A mortar.	The tongue.
Page 109.	Page 110.	Page 110.	Page 110.	Page 110.
136. 舛	137. 舟	138. 艮	139. 色	140. 艸
Sen.	Shū.	Kon, gon.	Shoku, shiki.	Sō.
Somuku.	Fune.	Todomaru, kagiru, katai.	Iro.	Kusa.
To oppose.	A boat.	To stop, limit, hard.	Colour.	Grass. (艹 Sō-kō.)
Page 110.	Page 111.	Page 111.	Page 111.	Page 112.
141. 虍	142. 虫	143. 血	144. 行	145. 衣
Ko.	Ki.	Ketsu.	Kō, giō.	I.
(Tora-kammuri.) Tora.	(Mushi-hen.) Mushi, hebi.	Chi.	Yuku.	Koromo.
A tiger.	An insect, reptile.	Blood.	To go.	Clothing. (衤 Koromo hen.)
Page 115.	Page 116.	Page 117.	Page 117.	Page 118.
146. 襾	147. 見	148. 角	149. 言	150. 谷
A, ka.	Ken.	Kaku.	Gen, gon. (Gom-ben.) Iu, kotoba.	Koku.
Ōu.	Miru.	Tsuno.		Tani.
To cover.	To see.	A horn.	To speak, a word.	A valley.
Page 119.	Page 119.	Page 119.	Page 120.	Page 124.

151. 豆 Tō, zu. *Mame.* A bean, pea. Page 124.	152. 豕 Shi. *Inoko, buta.* A pig. Page 124.	153. 豸 Chi. *Ashinakimushi, haumushi.* Reptiles. Page 124.	154. 貝 Bai, mai. *Kai.* A shell. Page 125.	155. 赤 Seki, shaku. *Akai.* Red. Page 126.	
156. 走 Sō. (*Sō-niū.*) *Washiru.* To run. Page 127.	157. 足 Soku. *Ashi.* A foot. Page 127.	158. 身 Shin. *Mi.* The body. Page 128.	159. 車 Sha. *Kuruma.* A wheel, carriage. Page 128.	160. 辛 Shin. *Karai.* Bitter. Page 129.	
161. 辰 Shin. *Tatsu, toki.* The "dragon," time. Page 129.	162. 辵 Chaku. *Washiru.* To go, run. (辶 *Shin-niu.*) Page 130.	163. 邑 Yū. *Ōzato, mura.* A village, city, capital. (阝 *Ozato-hen.*) Page 132.	164. 酉 Yū. *Tori, umu.* The "bird," satiated. Page 133.	165. 釆 Han, hen. *Wakatsu.* To divide. Page 134.	
166. 里 Ri. *Sato.* A village, Japanese or Chinese mile. Page 134.	167. 金 Kin, kon. *Kane.* Gold, metal, money. Page 134.	168. 長 Chō. *Nagai.* Long. Page 137.	169. 門 Mon. *Kado.* A gate. Page 137.	170. 阜 Fu, hiū. *Oka.* A mound. (阝 *Kozato-hen.*) Page 138.	
171. 隶 Tai. *Oyobu.* To reach. Page 139.	172. 隹 Sui. *Furutori.* Birds. Page 139.	173. 雨 U. *Ame.* Rain. Page 140.	174. 靑 Sei. *Aoi.* Green, azure. Page 141.	175. 非 Hi. *Arazu.* Not. Page 141.	
176. 面 Men. *Omote, kawo.* Face, front. Page 141.	177. 革 Kaku. *Kawa.* Hide, leather. Page 142.	178. 韋 I. *Oshikawa, somuku.* Tanned and soft leather, to oppose. Page 142.	179. 韭 Kiū. *Nira.* A leek. Page 142.	180. 音 In, on. *Koe, oto.* Voice, sound. Page 142.	

181. 頁	182. 風	183. 飛	184. 食	185. 首
KETSU.	FŪ.	HI.	SHOKU, JIKI.	SHU, SHŪ.
Kashira, kōbe.	Kaze.	Tobu.	Meshi, kū.	Kōbe.
The head.	Wind.	To fly.	Boiled rice, to eat.	The head.
Page 142.	Page 143.	Page 144.	Page 144.	Page 145.

186. 香	187. 馬	188. 骨	189. 高	190. 髟
KŌ.	BA, ME.	KOTSU.	KŌ.	HIŌ.
Nioi.	Uma.	Hone.	Takai.	Nagai kami no ke.
Odour, incense.	A horse.	A bone.	High.	Long hair.
Page 145.	Page 145.	Page 146.	Page 146.	Page 146.

191. 鬥	192. 鬯	193. 鬲	194. 鬼	195. 魚
TŌ.	CHŌ.	REKI, KAKU.	KI.	GIO.
Tatakau.	Kaorigusa.	Ashiganae.	Oni.	Uo.
To fight.	Fragrant herbs.	A tripod.	A spirit, ghost, devil.	A fish.
Page 147.	Page 147.	Page 147.	Page 147.	Page 148.

196. 鳥	197. 鹵	198. 鹿	199. 麥	200. 麻
CHŌ.	RO.	ROKU.	BAKU.	MA.
Tori.	Shiohama.	Shika.	Mugi.	Asa.
A bird.	A salt beach, salt.	A deer.	Wheat.	Hemp.
Page 149.	Page 150.	Page 150.	Page 150.	Page 150.

201. 黃	202. 黍	203. 黑	204. 黹	205. 黽
KWŌ, Ō.	SHO.	KOKU.	CHI.	BIN, BŌ.
Ki.	Kibi.	Kuroi.	Nuimono.	Kaeru.
Yellow.	Millet.	Black.	Embroidery.	A frog, toad.
Page 151.	Page 151.	Page 151.	Page 151.	Page 151.

206. 鼎	207. 鼓	208. 鼠	209. 鼻	210. 齊
TEI, CHŌ.	KO, KU.	SO, SHO.	BI.	SEI.
Kanae.	Tsuzumi.	Nezumi.	Hana.	Hitoshii.
A tripod.	A drum.	A rat, mouse.	The nose.	Alike, even.
Page 152.	Page 152.	Page 152.	Page 152.	Page 152.

211. 齒	212. 龍	213. 龜	214. 龠
SHI.	RIŌ, RIŬ.	KI.	YAKU.
Ha, yowai.	*Tatsu.*	*Kame.*	*Fue.*
Teeth, age.	A dragon, imperial.	A tortoise.	A flute.
Page 152.	Page 153.	Page 153.	Page 153.

Nanori ... ... Page 155.	Government Offices ... ... Page 163.
Provinces of Japan ... ... Page 159.	Names of Countries, &c. ... ... Page 163.
Fu and *Ken* of Japan ... ... Page 162.	

一 ✕	丁 ✕	七 ✕	丈 ✕	三 ✕
(The 1st Radical) ITSU, ICHI. *Hitotsu, kazu.* One.	TEI, CHŌ. *Hinoto, waLōdo, yoboro.* The fourth calendar sign, an adult, servant, a measure of length, 1/36 of a ri.	SHICHI. *Nanatsu.* Seven.	JŌ. *Take.* Ten *shaku* (about 10 English feet), measure, stature, quantity, an elder, Mr.	SAN. *Mitsu.* Three.
上 ✕	下 ✕	不 ✕	丐 ✕	丑 ✕
JŌ. *Ue, kami, noboru, agaru.* Above, high, superior, first, to ascend, send up.	GE, KA. *Shita, shimo, kudaru, sagaru.* Below, inferior, lowest, to descend, send down.	FŪ, FU. *Zu, ina.* Not, a negative verbal suffix.	KAI, KATSU. *Kou, atau.* To beg, bestow, a beggar.	CHŪ. *Ushi.* The ox, (the 2nd of the twelve horary characters), from 2 till 4 o'clock a.m.
且 ✕	丕	世 ✕	丘 ✕	丙 ✕
SHO, SHA. *Shibaraku, mata, katsu, karisome,* For a short time, again, moreover, supposing that.	HI. *Ōi naru.* Large, great, unequalled.	SE, SEI. *Yo.* The world, age, times, generation.	KIŪ. *Oka.* A mound, Confucius.	HEI. *Hinoe.* The third of the ten calendar signs, third, C.
丞	並 ✕			
JŌ. *Tasukeru, tsugu, ukeru.* To assist, connect, receive, an old man (used in plays), an assistant official of high rank.	NARABU, NARABI, awaseru. To be arranged in a row, together with, to unite.			
丨	中 ✕	串 ✕		
(The 2nd Radical) KON. *Tate, susumu, shirizoku.* A connecting line perpendicularly, to pass through.	CHŪ. *Naka, nakaba, uchi, ataru.* The inside, centre, within, to hit, correspond with.	KWAN. *Tsuranuku, kushi.* To string together, a skewer.		
丶	丸 ✕	丹 ✕	主 ✕	
(The 3rd Radical) CHU. *Shirushi.* A mark, point.	GWAN. *Marui, maru.* Round, a circle, a pill, used in the names of ships, etc.	TAN. *Akai.* Red, a pill, bullet, or anything round.	SHU. *Aruji, tsukasa, tsukasadoru, omonaru.* A lord, ruler, to rule, principal.	

ノ	ノ	乂	乃	久	之
	(The 4th Radical) HETSU. *Hidari e modoru.* A stroke to the left.	GAI. *Karu, osameru.* To cut (grass), govern.	NAI, DAI. *Nanji, sunawachi.* You, that is, namely, then.	KIŪ. *Hisashii, nagai.* A long time, lasting.	SHI. *No, kore, yuku.* Of, this, to go.
	乎 KO. *Ka, ou, ya.* An interrogative particle, an interjection betokening sadness.	乏 BŌ. *Toboshii.* Poor, deficient, lacking.	乍 SA. *Niwaka, tachi-machi, nagara.* Suddenly, forthwith, while.	乖 KWAI. *Somuku, tagau.* To disobey, oppose.	乘 JŌ. *Noru, noboru.* To ride, ascend.
乙	乙 (The 5th Radical) ITSU, OTSU. *Kinoto.* The second of the ten calendar signs, second, inferior, B.	九 KIU, KU. *Kokonotsu.* Nine.	乞 KITSU. *Kou, motomeru.* To beg, request.	也 YA. *Nari, mata.* It is, a verbal form used to complete a sentence, (frequently, without meaning), again.	乳 NIŪ. *Chichi.* Milk.
	乾 KEN, KAN. *Inui, ame, kawaku.* The North West, the Heavens, dry.	亂 RAN. *Midareru.* To be disordered, thrown into confusion.			
亅	(The 6th Radical) KETSU. *Kagi.* A hook, to mark off.	了 RYŌ. *Owaru, satoru.* To finish, understand.	予 YO. *Ware, ataeru.* I, one's self, one's own, to give.	事 JI. *Koto, shiwaza, tsukaeru.* A thing, deed, work, to serve, manage.	
二	(The 7th Radical) JI, NI. *Futatsu.* Two.	于 U. *Koko ni, oite, ni, yuku.* Here, in, at, as to, to go.	云 UN. *Iu, iwaku.* To say, speak.	互 GO. *Tagai ni, kawaru gawaru.* Mutually.	五 GO. *Itsutsu.* Five.

井 ヰ	亙 ヰ	況 キ	些 サ	亞 ア
SEI.	Kō.	Kiō.	SA, SHA.	A.
I, ido.	*Wataru, watari, amaneku.*	*Iwanya, koko ni.*	*Sukoshi.*	*Tsugu, tsugi, minikui, ashii.*
A well.	To cross over, the distance across, universally.	Much more, here, furthermore.	A little.	To succeed, next, ugly, bad.

亟				
KIOKU.				
Sumiyaka, shibashiba.				
Quick, frequently.				

亠	亡 ヰ	市 ヰ	交 ヰ	亥 ヰ
(The 8th Radical)	Bō, Mō.	SHI.	Kō.	GAI.
TŌ.	*Shinu, horobu, ushinau nigeru.*	*Ichi, kau, uru.*	*Majiwaru, majieru, tagai ni, komoyomo.*	I.
Futa.				
A cover. (This radical is always placed on the top.)	To die, be destroyed, lose, run away.	A market, to buy, sell, a town.	To associate with, mix, mutually, by turns.	The "hog," the last of the twelve horary characters.

亦 ヰ	亨 ヰ	享 ヰ	京 ヰ	亭 ヰ
EKI.	Kiō, Kō.	Kiō.	Kiō, KEI.	TEI.
Mata.	*Tōru.*	*Matsuru, ukeru.*	*Miyako, ōi naru, takai.*	*Hitoya, azumaya, todomaru, takai, tairaka.*
Again, moreover.	To pass through, pervade.	To worship, offer, sacrifice, receive.	A capital, great, high.	A shed, an arbour, to stop, high, level.

亮	商 ヰ			
RIŌ.	SHŌ.			
Hogaraka, makoto, tōru.	*Akinau, akinai, hakaru.*			
Clear, bright, truth.	To trade, commerce, to estimate.			

人 ヰ	什 ヰ	仁 ヰ	仄 ヰ	仆 ヰ	人
(The 9th Radical)	SHŪ, JŪ.	JIN, NIN.	SOKU.	FU.	
JIN, NIN.	*Tō.*	*Itsukushimu, awaremu, hito.*	*Katamuku, iyashii.*	*Taoru.*	
Hito, tami.					
A man, person, human.	Ten, a file of ten soldiers, household furniture.	To love, pity, humanity.	To lean to one side, low, the oblique tones of Chinese words.	To fall over.	

他	仗	付	仔	仙
TA.	Jō.	FU, FŪ.	SHI.	SEN.
Hoka.	*Mamoru, yoru, tsue.*	*Tsuku, tsukeru, sazukeru.*	*Taeru, katsu.*	*Yamabito, hijiri.*
Other, another, that.	To guard, depend on, a cane.	To adhere to, refer to, apply, give.	To bear, sustain, attentive.	A fairy, hermit.
仞	代	令	以	仲
JIN.	DAI.	REI, RIŌ.	I.	CHŪ.
Hiro.	*Yo, kawari, kawarugawaru.*	*Nori, yoi, seshi-muru.*	*Motte, omommiru.*	*Naka.*
A fathom, full.	Generation, reign, a substitute, representative, instead of, by turns.	A rule, order, command, good, to cause to do.	By, on account of, with, to consider.	The middle.
企	件	伍	伏	伉
KI.	KEN.	GO.	FUKU.	KŌ.
Kuwadateru, tsu-mudateru, nozomu.	*Kudan, wakatsu.*	*Itsutari, narabu.*	*Fusu, kakureru.*	*Au, ataru, tagui.*
To plot, plan, stand on tiptoe, expect.	Matter, affair, above mentioned, to divide.	A file of five men, to be arranged in a row.	To bend down, lie down, be concealed.	To compare, match, a married pair.
任	伎	仰	伐	伊
NIN.	GI.	GIŌ.	BATSU.	I.
Makaseru, taeru, ninau.	*Takumi, waza.*	*Aogu, aomuku.*	*Utsu, kiru.*	*Kore, tada.*
Trust, appointment, duty, to entrust with, endure, bear.	Skill, ability.	To look upwards, respect.	To strike, cut, kill.	This, only.
休	佃	何	作	伶

佇 ✕ Cho. *Tatazumu.* To stand still.	估 ✕ Ko. *Uru, atai.* To sell, value.	佚 ✕ Itsu. *Tanoshimu, yasunzuru.* Ease, idle, leisure.	位 ✕ I. *Kurai.* Rank, kind, quantity, position, standard.
伯 ✕ Haku. *ni, oji, tsukasa.* n elder brother, lor, uncle, count, official.	伺 ✕ Shi. *Ukagau.* To enquire, examine carefully, spy.	仲 ✕ Shin. *Nobiru, nobasu.* To stretch.	但 ✕ Tan. *Tada, tadashi.* But, however, only, (used in introducing an explanatory note.)
作 ✕ Saku. *nukuru, nasu.* To build, make, perform.	似 ✕ Ji. *Niru, shimesu.* To resemble, show forth.	佑 ✕ Yū. *Tasukeru, suke.* To assist, aid.	佛 ✕ Futsu, butsu. *Hotoke.* Buddha.
低 ✕ Tei. *Hikui.* Low.	佞 ✕ Nei. *Hetsurau.* To flatter, persuasive, artful.	伴 ✕ Yō. *Itsuwaru.* To lie, cheat.	佶 ✕ Kitsu. *Sukoyaka, tadashii.* Robust, correct.
使 ✕ Shi. *tsukai, tsukau, seshimeru.* A messenger, to by on official commissions, cause to do.	侍 ✕ Ji. *Haberu, samurau.* To attend upon, serve.	併 ✕ Hei. *Narabu, awaseru, narabi ni.* To be arranged in order, unite, together with.	舍 ✕ Sha. *Ie, yadoru.* A house, to lodge.
依 ✕ I. *Yoru, yotte.* To depend upon, rding to, owing to, by, therefore.	侈 ✕ Shi. *Ogoru.* To be extravagant, profuse.	例 ✕ Rei. *Tameshi, tagui, tsuranaru.* A precedent, kind, to be arranged.	佳 ✕ Ka. *Yoi, utsukushii.* Good, beautiful, felicitous.

(14)

來 *	侮 *	俘 *	俟 *	信 *
Rai.	Bu.	Fu.	Shi.	Shin.
Kitaru, kuru, itaru.	Anadoru.	Toriko.	Matsu.	Makoto, otozure, noberu.
To come, reach, next.	To despise.	A captive.	To wait.	To believe, truth, tidings, to relate.
侯 *	侶 *	俑 *	便 *	俚 *
Kō.	Rio.	Yō.	Ben, bin.	Ri.
Kimi, ukagau.	Tomo, tomogara.	Hitogata.	Tsugō, tayori, sunawachi.	Iyashii.
A lord, marquis, to enquire after, hope for.	A companion.	An image, statue.	Opportunity, convenient, tidings, that is.	Low, vulgar, rustic.
促 *	俄 *	係 *	保 *	俗 *
Soku.	Ga.	Kei.	Hō, ho.	Zoku.
Unagasu, semaru.	Niwaka.	Kakaru, kakawaru, tsunagu.	Tamotsu, mamoru, yasunzuru.	Narawashi.
To urge, dun.	Suddenly.	To concern, relate to, bind.	To protect, preserve, tranquillize.	Custom, common, secular.
俠 *	俾 *	俊 *	俞 *	侵 *
Kiō.	Hi.	Shun.	Yu.	Shin.
Otokodate.	Masu, shitagau, seshimeru.	Sugureru.	Iyoiyo, shikari to su.	Okasu.
A chivalrous person, helper of the oppressed.	To increase, obey, cause to do.	To excel, eminent.	More and more, certainly, to assent.	To attack, violate, brave.
俎 *	俩 *	俳 *	俏 *	倫 *
So.	Riō.	Hai.	Shō.	Rin.
Manaita.	Takumi.	Tachimodoru, tawamure.	Izanau, tanoshimu.	Tagui, hitoshii, tsune, michi.
A 3 legged basin, chopping board.	Clever, skilled.	To go to and fro, sport, play.	To allure, seduce, rejoice.	Sort, alike, in classes, usual, the right way, principle, natural relationships.
傚 *	俸 *	倅 *	倍 *	倭 *
Hō.	Hō.	Sai, sui.	Bai.	I, wa.
Narau.	Tamamono.	Segare, soeru.	Masumasu, masu.	Yamato, shitagau, tsutsushimu.
To imitate.	Salary.	Son (one's own), to add, supplement.	More and more, to increase, double.	Japan, (used disrespectfully), to obey, be respectful.

倒 ✗ **Tō.** *Taoru, sakashima.* To fall down, upside down.	倖 ✗ **Kō.** *Saiwai.* Happiness.	俺 **En.** *Ware.* I, myself.	借 ✗ **Shaku.** *Kariru, kari ni.* To borrow, rent, temporarily.	値 ✗ **Chi.** *Neuchi, atai.* Value.
俵 ✗ **Hiō.** *Tawara.* A straw-bag.	倩 **Sen.** *Tsuratsura, utsukushii.* Carefully, attentively, beautiful.	俱 ✗ **Gu.** *Tomo ni, mina.* Together, all.	倉 ✗ **Sō.** *Kura.* A godown.	俶 **Shuku.** *Hajime, yoi, sugureru.* The beginning, good, excellent.
俯 ✗ **Fu.** *Utsumuku.* To look down, turn upside down.	倦 ✗ **Ken.** *Umu.* To be tired of.	修 ✗ **Shū.** *Totonou, osameru, nagai.* To arrange, renovate, repair, practice, long.	倏 **Shuku.** *Tachimachi, sumiyaka.* Suddenly, quick.	倨 **Kio.** *Ogoru.* To be proud.
候 ✗ **Kō.** *Ukagau, matsu, sōrō.* To enquire after, be a candidate for, wait, to be (an auxiliary verb used in the written language.)	偕 ✗ **Kai.** *Tomo ni, tsuyoi.* Together, strong.	偏 ✗ **Hen.** *Katayoru, iyashii, hitoe ni.* To incline, partial, mean, rustic, wholly, earnestly.	偶 ✗ **Gū.** *Tamatama, narabu, hitogata.* Occasionally, to be arranged in order, an image, an even number.	健 ✗ **Ken.** *Sukoyaka, tsuyoi.* Healthy, strong.
倚 **I.** *Yoru, tanomu, katayoru.* To rely on, incline.	偸 **Tō.** *Nusumu, hisoka ni.* To steal, secretly.	假 ✗ **Ka.** *Karu, kari ni.* To borrow, temporarily.	偵 **Tei.** *Ukagau, saguru.* To inquire after, spy, detect.	側 ✗ **Soku.** *Kawa, soba, katawara, katamuku.* The side, one side, to incline to one side.
偃 **En.** *Fuseru, taoreru, ikou.* To lie prostrate, fall over, rest.	偈 **Ge, ketsu.** *Sumiyaka.* Buddhist verses, quick.	偉 ✗ **I.** *Ōi naru.* Large, great, admirable.	偖 ✗ **Sha.** *Sate.* Well, so then, (used at the beginning of a sentence.)	做 ✗ **Sa.** *Nasu.* To do, act.

停 ✗	傅 ✗	傑 ✗	備 ✗	傍 ✗
TEI.	FU.	KETSU.	BI.	HŌ, BŌ.
Todomeru.	Kashizuku, tasukeru.	Sugureru.	Sonaeru, sonawaru.	Katawara, hotori.
To stop.	To wait on, nurse, assist.	To excel.	To offer, prepare, be endowed with.	The side, one side.

倣	傘 ✗	傲	催 ✗	傾 ✗
KŌ.	SAN.	GŌ.	SAI.	KEI.
Narau, nottoru.	Karakasa.	Ogoru, anadoru.	Moyōsu, semaru.	Katamuku, katamukeru.
To imitate.	An umbrella.	To be proud, despise.	To make, prepare, urge.	To incline to one side, be biassed, subvert.

僂	傷 ✗	傳 ✗	僅 ✗	僉
RŌ, RU.	SHŌ.	DEN.	KIN.	SEN.
Semushi, semushigamai.	Itamu, kizutsukeru.	Tsutaeru.	Wazuka.	Mina, kotogotoku.
A hunchback, the back bent (as with rheumatism).	To hurt, injure, wound.	To hand on, transmit from one to another, tradition.	Little.	All, the whole.

傭 ✗	債 ✗	僥 ✗	僦 ✗	僕 ✗
YŌ.	SAI.	GIŌ.	SHŪ.	BOKU.
Yatou.	Oime, hataru.	Itsuwaru.	Kariru, yatou.	Shimobe.
To employ, an employee.	Debt, to demand payment.	To lie, unexpected.	To borrow, employ, hire.	A servant, I.

僑	僧 ✗	僮	僚	像 ✗
KIŌ.	SŌ.	DŌ.	RIŌ.	ZŌ.
Yadoru.	Yosutebito.	Warabe, shimobe.	Tomogara, tsukaebito.	Katachi, katadoru.
To reside temporarily, lodge.	A hermit, a Buddhist priest.	A child, boy, servant.	A colleague, companion, an employee (official or other).	An image, to shape like.

僞 ✗	僭	僻 ✗	儂	僵
GI.	SEN.	HEKI.	NŌ.	KIŌ.
Itsuwari.	Itsuwaru, (hitokoroi).	Higamu, katayoru.	Ware, kare.	Taoreru.
A lie.	To lie, arrogate to one's self what belongs to some one else.	To be warped, prejudiced, mean, remote.	I, he.	To lie down, be stretched out.

億 OKU. *Hakaru.* One hundred million, to measure.	儉 KEN. *Tsuzumayaka.* Economical.	價 KA. *Atai.* Value.	儀 GI. *Nori, yoshi.* A rule, ceremony, good, an affair.	儔 CHŪ. *Tomogara, tagui, hitoshii.* Companions, kind, like.
儒 JU. *Hakase.* A sage, scholar, Confucianist.	儘 JIN. *Mama, mina.* Condition, all.	償 SHŌ. *Tsukunou.* To compensate, redeem, indemnify.	優 YŪ. *Yawaraka, yutaka, tawamure.* Soft, amiable, rich, abundant, act, play.	儲 CHO. *Mōke, takuwaeru.* Provisions, stores, to lay up.
儺 DA. *Oniyarai.* The ceremony of driving out evil spirits.	儼 GEN. *Ogosoka.* Fine, majestic.			

儿 (The 10th Radical) JIN. *Hito.* A man, person, the people, human.	兀 KOTSU, GOTSU. *Kaburo, hageru.* Bald.	允 IN. *Ataru, makoto.* To conform to, truth.	元 GEN, GWAN. *Moto, hajime, tsukasa, kōbe.* Origin, beginning, ruler, head, principal.	兄 KEI. *Ani, konokami.* An elder brother.	儿
充 JŪ. *Michiru.* To be full, complete.	兆 CHŌ. *Kizashi, urakata.* A billion, a sign, omen (as in divination).	兇 KIŌ. *Ashi', arai, osoreru.* Evil, rough, to fear.	先 SEN. *Sak', mazu, haj'me, moto, susumu, sakinjiru.* The front, before, well, future, past, beginning, origin, to advance, put first.	光 KWŌ. *Teru, hikari.* To shine, light.	
克 KOKU. *Katsu, yoku suru.* To conquer, be able.	兌 DA. *Yorokobu, kaeru.* To rejoice, exchange.	免 BEN, MEN. *Manukareru, yurusu, shirizokeru.* To escape, exempt, pardon, permit, send away.	兒 JI, NI. *Chigo, ko.* A child, infant.	兎 TO. *Usagi.* A rabbit.	

	兜 × Tō. *Kabuto.* A helmet.	競 × Kiō. *Kisou, osoreru.* To emulate, compete, fear.			
入	入 × (The 11th Radical). Jū, niū. *Iru.* To enter.	内 × Nai. *Uchi, ireru.* Inside, among, the Imperial Palace, to put in.	全 × Zen. *Mattai, sonawaru.* Whole, complete, to be endowed with.	兩 × Riō. *Fntatsu, futatabi.* Two, both, twice, a *riō*, (a dollar, a tael.)	
八	八 × (The 12th Radical). Hatsu, hachi. *Yatsu.* Eight.	公 × Kō, ku. *Ōyake, kimi, tsukasa.* Public, just, a duke, ruler.	六 × Riku, roku. *Mtsu.* Six.	共 × Kiō. *Tomo ni, mina, awaseru, domo.* Together with, all, to unite, but.	兵 × Hei, hiō. *Tsuwamono, hamono.* A soldier, troops, weapons.
	其 × Ki. *Sore, sono.* That.	具 × Gu. *Sonaeru, sonawaru, tsubusa ni, tomo ni.* To offer (to a superior), provide, be endowed with, minutely, together, a complete set of furniture, etc.	典 × Ten. *Nori, tsukasadoru.* Statute, records, a rule, to manage, a lexicon.	兼 × Ken. *Kaneru, awaseru.* To do two things or discharge two duties at once, unite.	異 × I. *Kotonaru, ayashii.* To differ, strange, foreign.
	冀 × Ki. *Koi negau, nozomu.* To desire eagerly, pray for, hope.				
冂	冂 (The 13th Radical). Kei. *Maki.* A border, limit.	册 × Saku, satsu. *Fuda, shigarami.* A ticket, volume, an embankment, (of piles, &c.)	再 × Sai. *Mata, futatabi.* Again, twice.	冏 × Kei. *Akiraka, hikari.* Clear, light.	冑 × Chū. *Kabuto.* A helmet.

冗 Jō. *Amaru.* exceed, be superfluous, mixed up.	冠 Kwan. *Kammuri, kaburu.* A head-covering, cap, crown, to put on the head.	冢 Chō. *Tsuka.* A mound, chief.	冥 Mei, Miō. *Kasuka, kurai, fukai.* Dim, dark, deep, Hades.
冬 Tō. *Fuyu.* Winter.	冰 Hiō. *Kōri, kōru.* Ice, to freeze.	冱 Go. *Hieru, kogoeru.* To be cold, frozen.	冲 Chū. *Itokenai.* Young.
凌 Riō. *Kōri, shinogu.* Ice, to brave, endure.	冷 Rei. *Samui, tsumetai, suzushii, hiyayaka.* Cold, cool.	列 Retsu. *Hageshii, samui.* Severe, cold.	凋 Chō. *Shibomu, sokonau.* To close, wither, injure.
凉 Riō. *Suzushii.* Cool, refreshing.	凄 Sei. *Samui, sugoi, susamashii.* Cold, dreary, horrible.	凝 Giō. *Kōru, katamaru.* To freeze, harden.	凛 Rin. *Samui, susamashii.* Cold, fearful, dreary.

	凱 GAI. *Yoi, tanoshimu.* Good, to rejoice, be victorious.				
凵	凵 (The 17th Radical) KAN. *Kuchi heru.* A receptacle, to open the mouth.	凶 ✛ KIŌ. *Ashii, wazawai.* Evil, misfortune.	凸 ✛ TOTSU. *Deru, nakadokoro.* To portrude, convex.	凹 ✛ Ō. *Nakakubo.* Concave.	出 ✛ SHUTSU, SUI. *Deru, dasu.* To go out, put out.
	函 ✛ KAN. *Hako.* A box.				
刀 刂	刀 ✛ (The 18th Radical) TŌ. *Katana.* A sword.	刃 ✛ JIN, NIN. *Yaiba, ha.* The blade or edge of a sword or other sharp instrument, an edged weapon, sword.	刈 ✛ KAI, GAI. *Kiru, karu.* To cut (as grain), reap.	分 ✛ FUN, BUN. *Wakachi, wakeru, wakaru.* A part, share, rate, duty, to divide, understand, a minute, a fun, (5.80 grs. Troy.)	切 ✛ SETSU, SAI. *Kiru, kizamu, semeru, shikiri ni.* To cut, chop up, carve, press upon, constantly.
	刊 ✛ KAN. *Kiru, kizamu.* To cut, carve, engrave, print, publish.	刑 ✛ KEI. *Nori, tsumi naru, korosu.* A rule, to punish, kill.	列 ✛ RETSU. *Tsuide, kumi, tsuraneru.* Rank, order, to arrange in a row.	刎 ✛ FUN. *Kiru, kubihaneru.* To cut, cut off the head.	別 ✛ BETSU. *Hanareru, wakeru.* To separate, differ, divide, distinguish, another.

初 ケ Sho. *Hajime, moto.* The beginning, origin.	**利** リ Ri. *Toshi, yoi, musaboru.* Interest, profit, victory, quick, good, to covet.	**判** ケ Han. *Wakatsu, wakeru, kotowaru.* A seal, stamp, to divide, judge.	**删** San. *Kezuru.* To pare off.	**制** ケ Sei, sai. *Nori, tsukuru, tadasu, osameru, tomeru.* A rule, instructions, uniform, fixed, to make, rectify, govern, stop.
券 ケ Ken. *Warifu, tegata.* A tally, ticket, deed, note, certificate.	**刻** ケ Koku. *Kizamu, kiru.* To carve, engrave, cut, a period of time.	**刮** Kwatsu. *Kezuru, suru.* To scrape, rub.	**刳** Ko. *Waru, kubomeru, hofuru.* To divide, hollow out, split, cut in pieces.	**刷** ケ Satsu. *Suru, kiru, kezuru, harau.* To rub, cut, pare off, print, clear away.
刺 ケ Shi. *Korosu, sasu, soshiru.* To kill, stick, stab, slander.	**刹** ケ Satsu. *Hashira, tera.* A pillar, Buddhist temple.	**到** ケ Tō. *Itaru.* To reach.	**剃** ケ Tei. *Soru.* To shave.	**削** ケ Saku. *Kezuru.* To scrape, cut off, take away.
則 ケ Soku. *Nori, nottoru, sunawachi.* A rule, to imitate, that is.	**前** ケ Zen. *Mae, moto, saki, susumu.* Before, the front, former, in the presence of, to advance.	**剄** Kei. *Kubihaneru.* To cut off the head.	**剋** ケ Koku. *Katsu, korosu.* To conquer, kill.	**剝** ケ Haku. *Hagu, otosu.* To flay, deprive of, degrade.
剖 ケ Hō, bō. *Saku, waru, wakatsu.* To tear asunder, divide, dissect.	**剛** ケ Gō. *Katai, tsuyoi, kowai, takei.* Hard, strong, valiant.	**剚** Ji. *Sashihasamu, oku.* To insert, transfix.	**剪** Shin. *Hasamu, kiru.* To cut with scissors, cut.	**副** ケ Fuku. *Sou, tasukeru.* To be along with, assist, assistant, vice (used in official titles.)
剩 ケ Jō. *Amaru, amassae.* To exceed, be left over, moreover.	**割** ケ Katsu. *Saku, waru, sokonau.* To tear, divide, injure, a share, dividend, per centage.	**創** ケ Sō. *Kizu, kizutsukeru, hajime.* A wound, to wound, the beginning.	**劆** Tō. *Kagi, kama.* A hook, sickle.	**剿** ケ Shō, sō. *Tatsu, korosu.* To cut, destroy, attack and fight rebels.

(21)

劉	割	罰	劈	劇
RIKU.	KWAKU, KAKU.	BATSU.	HEKI, HAKU.	GEKI.
Korosu.	Kagiru, sogu, kizamu.	Tsumi suru, tsumi nasu.	Saku, tsunzaku.	Hanahada, hageshii, masu, tawamureru.
To kill.	To limit, slice off, carve.	Punishment, to punish.	To tear, rend asunder.	Very, violent, to increase, play (as in a theatre).
劍	劑			
KEN.	ZAI.			
Tsurugi.	Awaseru, totonoeru, hitoshiku suru.			
A sword, broad-word.	To unite, compound (medicines), make alike.			

力

力	功	加	劣	劫
(The 19th Radical) RIKI, RIOKU.	KŌ.	KA.	RETSU.	KŌ, GŌ.
Chikara, tsutomeru.	Isaoshi.	Masu, kuwaeru.	Otoru.	Kasumetoru, obiyakasu.
Strength, power, force, to exert one's self.	Merit, ability, efficacy.	To increase, add to.	To be inferior.	To take by force, frighten.
助	努	効	劾	勇
JO.	DO.	KŌ.	GAI.	YŪ.
Tasukeru, sukeru.	Hagemu, tsutomeru.	Shirushi, narau.	Tsutomeru, kiwameru.	Isameru, tsuyoi, takei.
To assist, rescue.	To exert one's self, labour.	Effect, merit, result, to imitate.	To exert one's self, investigate carefully.	To inspirit, strong, valiant.
勃	勉	勁	勅	動
BOTSU.	BEN.	KEI.	CHOKU.	DŌ.
Niwaka, okoru.	Tsutomeru, hagemu, susumeru.	Tsuyoi, sukoyaka, katai.	Mikotonori.	Ugoku, yayamosureba.
Suddenly, to rise.	To labour, exert one's self, exhort.	Strong, healthy, hard.	An Imperial decree.	To move, liable to.
勒	務	勘	勗	勝
ROKU.	MU.	KAN.	KIOKU.	SHŌ.
Osaeru, kizamu.	Tsutomeru, tsutome.	Sadamaru, kanyaeru.	Tsutomeru.	Katsu, masaru, sugureru, taeru.
A bridle, to restrain, engrave.	To labour, perform official duty, service, business.	To settle, consider.	To exert one's self, labour diligently.	To conquer, surpass, excel, endure.

(23)

勞 ✕	勣	勢	勤 ✕	募 ✕
Rō.	Seki.	Sei.	Kin.	Bo.
Tsukareru, tsutomeru, isaoshi, itawaru.	Isaoshi.	Ikioi.	Tsutomeru, nengoro.	Tsunoru, motomeru.
To be weary, labour, trouble, merit, to pity, care for.	Merit.	Power, force, condition.	To labour, serve, careful, kind.	To raise, levy, obtain.
勳 ✕	勵 ✕	勸 ✕		
Kun.	Rei.	Kwan, ken.		
Isaoshi.	Hagemu, tsutomeru, susumu.	Tsutomeru, tasukeru, susumeru.		
Merit.	To labour, exert one's self, encourage.	To labour, resist, encourage.		
勹	勺 ✕	勿 ✕	包 ✕	匍 ✕
The 20th Radical) Hō.	Shaku, seki.	Futsu.	Hō.	Ho.
Tsutsumu.	A measure of capacity, the 10th part of a gō, (about half an ounce Imperial measure).	Nakare, nashi.	Tsutsumu, kaneru.	Harabau.
To wrap up, envelope.		Do not, not.	To wrap up, envelope, contain, include two or more things in one.	To lie on the belly, creep.
匐				
Fuku.				
Harabau.				
To lie on the belly, creep.				
匕 ✕	化 ✕	北 ✕	匙 ✕	
The 21st Radical) Hi. Saji.	Kwa, ke.	Hoku.	Shi.	
	Kawaru, bake, bakeru.	Kita, nigeru, somuku.	Saji.	
A spoon.	To change, transform, a fraud, ghost.	The North, to run away, disobey.	A spoon.	
匚	匠 ✕	匡	匣	匪
The 22nd Radical) Hō.	Shō.	Kiō.	Kō.	Hi.
Mono wo ukeru utsuwa.	Takumi.	Hako, tadasu, tasukeru.	Hako.	Arazu.
A box, receptacle, an open basket with handle.	A carpenter, an expert, master.	A box, to correct, assist.	A box.	Not, vagabonds, rebels.

匡 Kɪ. *Hako.* A box.				
匚 The 23rd Radical Kei. *Kakusu, kakomi.* A case, coffer, to conceal, an enclosure.	匹 Hitsu. *Hiki, tagui, tomogara.* Numeral for animals, cash, hauls, a pair.	匿 Joku, toku. *Kakusu, nigeru.* To conceal, run away.	區 Ku. *Wakachi, machimachi, kakusu.* A division, distinction, district, various, to conceal.	
十 The 24th Radical) Jitsu, jū, shū. *Tō, tsuzu.* Ten.	千 Sen. *Chiji.* A thousand.	廾 Jū. *Hatachi (nijū).* Twenty.	卅 Sō. *Misoji (sanjū).* Thirty.	升 Shō. *Masu, noboru.* A *shō*, (a measure containing 109.375 cubic inches), to ascend.
午 Go. *Uma.* The 7th of the twelve horary characters, "the horse," twelve o'clock noon.	半 Han. *Nakaba, wakatsu.* The half, middle, to divide.	卑 Hi. *Iyashii, hikui.* Low, mean.	卒 Sotsu, shutsu. *Shimobe, moromoro, niwaka, owaru, tsukuru.* A servant, soldier, all, suddenly, to finish, graduate.	卓 Taku. *Takai.* High, eminent.
協 Kiō. *Kanau, tomo ni.* To suit, agree with, together, united.	南 Nan. *Minami.* The South.	博 Haku, baku. *Hiroi, amaneku.* Wide, everywhere, to gamble.		
卜 The 25th Radical) Boku. *Uranau.* To divine.	占 Sen. *Uranau, shimeru.* To divine, take possession of, seize.	卦 Ke, kei. *Urakata.* Signs of divination.		

卩 ✕ (The 26th Radical) SETSU. *Warifu.* A seal made in two parts that tally, a joint, knot.	卯 ✕ Bō. U. The 4th of the twelve horary characters, "the hare," six o'clock a.m.	印 ✕ IN. *Shirushi, oshide.* A sign, stamp, seal.	危 ✕ KI. *Ayaui, takai.* Dangerous, high.	却 ✕ KIAKU. *Shirizokeru, kaette* To refuse, send away, dismiss, on the contrary.
卵 ✕ RAN. *Tamago.* An egg.	卷 ✕ KEN, KWAN. *Maki, maku, fumi.* The numeral for rolls or volumes, a book, to roll up.	卸 ✕ SHA. *Orosu.* To let down, unload, sell at wholesale.	卽 ✕ SOKU. *Sunawachi, tsuku.* That is, then, forthwith, to follow, come in the place of, ascend (the throne).	卿 ✕ KEI, KIŌ. *Kimi, nanji.* A lord, the former Chief of a Department of State, you.
厂 ✕ The 27th Radical. GAN. *Iwao.* A cliff.	厄 ✕ YAKU. *Wazawai, kurushimu.* Calamity, misfortune, distressed.	厓 ✕ GAI. *Yamagiwa, mizugishi.* The edge of a hill, the water's edge, bank.	厚 ✕ KŌ. *Atsui.* Thick, great, kind, liberal.	原 ✕ GEN. *Hara, moto.* A moor, origin, source.
厥 ✕ KETSU. *Sono, mijikai.* That, these, short.	厦 ✕ KA, SA. *Ie.* A large house, mansion.	厭 ✕ EN. *Itou, akiru.* To be tired of, take care of, dislike, satisfied.	厲 ✕ REI. *Hageshii, eyami, togu.* Violent, pestilence, evil, to sharpen.	
厶 ✕ (The 28th Radical) SHI, DŌ. *Watakushi, kata mashii.* Private, selfish, depraved.	去 ✕ KIO. *Saru, hanareru.* To leave, go away, be separated from, reject, lost.	畚 ✕ HON. *Fugo.* A basket.	參 ✕ SAN. *Mairu, hakaru, majiwaru, azukaru.* To come, go, plan, mix with, visit (a temple etc.), take part in.	
又 ✕ (The 29th Radical) YŪ. *Mata.* Again.	叉 ✕ SA. *Komanuku, futamata.* To fold the hands, forked.	及 ✕ KIŪ. *Oyobu, itaru, tomo ni, oyobi.* To reach, arrive at, together with.	友 ✕ YŪ. *Tomo, mutsumajii.* A friend, companion, friendly.	反 ✕ HAN, HON. *Kaeru, kaesu, kaette, somuku.* To return, on the contrary, to disobey, rebel.

取 ⼈	受 ⼈	叛 ⼈	叟 ⼈
Shu.	Ju.	Han, hon.	Sō.
Toru.	Ukeru.	Somuku.	Toshiyori, okina.
To take, get.	To receive.	To disobey, rebel.	An old man, sir.
叢 ⼈			
Sō.			
Atsumeru, muragaru, kusamura.			
To collect, crowd together, a grassy place.			
古 ⼈	句 ⼈	叨 ⼈	叩 ⼈
Ko.	Kō, ku.	Tō.	Kō.
Furui, inishie.	Kagiru, magaru.	Midari ni.	Tataku, utsu.
Old, olden times.	A verse, sentence, to punctuate, stop.	Disorderly, improperly.	To beat, knock.
召 ⼈	叭 ⼈	叮 ⼈	可 ⼈
Shō.	Hatsu, hachi.	Tei.	Ka.
Mesu, yobu.	Kuchiakeru.	Nengoro.	Yoi, yurusu, beki.
To send for, call, summon.	To open the mouth, a sound.	Kind, polite.	Good, right, used as an auxiliary verb, to allow.
叱 ⼈	史 ⼈	右 ⼈	叶 ⼈
Shitsu.	Shi.	U, yū.	Kiō.
Shikaru.	Fumi, fubito.	Migi, tasukeru, tattobu.	Kanau.
To scold.	Annals, history, a historian.	The right (hand), the above, to honour, an official designation the 2nd official in rank.	To agree with, suit.
吁	吃	各	合
U.	Kitsu.	Kaku.	Gō, gatsu.
Aa.	Domoru.	Ono-ono.	Au, awaseru.
An interjection expressive of fear, sorrow, dislike.	To stammer.	Each, all, various.	To agree with, unite, a measure containing $5\frac{1}{16}$ ounces Imperial

吉	吋	同	名	后
KITSU, KICHI.	TŌ.	DŌ.	MEI, MIŌ.	KŌ.
Yoi.	—	*Onaji, tomo ni.*	*Na, nazukeru, homare.*	*Kimi, kisaki, nochi.*
Good, lucky.	An inch.	The same, together.	A name, to name, celebrated, used also as a numeral for human beings.	A Sovereign, Empress, after.

吏	吐	向	君	吝
RI.	TO.	KŌ, KIŌ.	KUN.	RIN.
Tsukasadoru.	*Haku.*	*Mukau, mukō, mukeru, saki ni.*	*Kimi, tattoi.*	*Oshimu, yabusaka.*
To rule, an official, officer.	To vomit, spit, utter.	To face, opposite to, to point to, the past.	A sovereign, lord, honourable, a gentleman, you.	To grudge, miserly.

呑	吟	吠	否	含
DON.	GIN.	HAI.	HI.	GAN.
Nomu, kuu.	*Nageku, utau, samayou.*	*Inu, hoeru.*	*Shikarazu, ina, ashii.*	*Fukumu.*
To drink, swallow.	To mourn, hum, wander about bewildered.	To bark.	Not so, no, bad.	To hold in the mouth, contain.

吭	呈	吳	吶	吸
KŌ.	TEI.	GO.	TOTSU.	KIU.
Nodobue.	*Shimesu, noberu, arawasu.*	*Kure, kamabisushii.*	*Nibui, domoru.*	*Sū, nomu.*
The windpipe.	To present (to a superior), state (to a superior), show.	Please, noisy, the name of an ancient Chinese state.	Slow (of speech), to stammer.	To suck, inhale, smoke.

吹	吻	吼	吾	告
SUI.	FUN.	KŌ, KU.	GO.	KŌ, KOKU.
Fuku.	*Kuchiwaki.*	*Ushinaku, hoeru.*	*Ware, waga.*	*Tsugeru, mikotonori.*
To blow.	The side of the mouth, lips.	To bellow, low, roar.	I, my, we, our.	To tell, inform, announce, an Imperial Order or official decree.

呂	叫	周	呪	味
RIO, RO.	KIŌ.	SHŪ.	SHU, JU.	MI.
Tsuranaru, sebone.	*Sakebu.*	*Meguru, amaneku, sukū.*	*Notto, norou, majinai.*	*Aji, ajiwai, ajiwau.*
To be arranged in a row, a keynote in music, backbone.	To cry out.	To go round, all, everywhere, to assist.	A Shinto prayer, to curse, a charm, spell.	Taste, to try, examine.

呻 Shin. Unaru, umeku. To moan, groan.	呼 Ko. Ikifuku, yobu. To expel the breath, breath out, call.	命 Mei. Inochi, mikoto, iitsuke, ōse. Life, an Imperial command, decree, fate.	呵 Ka. Semeru, warau, shikaru. To blame, laugh, scold.	咀 So. Kamu. To bite, chew, suck.
咄 Totsu. Tsubaki haku. hanashi. An interjection expressive of surprise.	和 Kwa, wa. Kaneu, totonou, yuwarayu, yamato. To agree with, be in harmony, tranquil, peace, Japan.	咕 Chō. Nameru, tsubuyaku. To lick, mutter to one's self.	告 Kiū. Togameru, toga. To blame, a crime, fault.	咨 Shi. Hakaru, koko, kore, aa. To plot, consult, here, this, an interjection expressive of sadness.
咫 Shi. Sukoshi. The distance of about a foot, close to, a little.	咲 Shō. Saku. To open (as a flower.)	咳 Gai. Seki. A cough.	咸 Kan. Mina, kotogotoku. All, entirely.	咽 In. Nondo, musebu. The throat, to be choked.
哀 Ai. Kanashimu, awaremu. To grieve, pity.	品 Hin. Shina. A thing, sort, circumstance, quality.	哂 Shin. Warau, azawarau. To laugh, laugh at.	哉 Sai. Kana, ka. A particle expressive of admiration, an interrogative particle.	哩 Ri. — A mile (English).
貞 In. Kazu. A numeral for men, a man, an official, member.	哥 Ka. Uta, utau. A song, to sing.	哭 Koku. Naku, sakebu. To weep, cry out, grieve.	唆 Sa. Magaru, odateru, keshikakeru. To be crooked, stir up, incite.	哮 Kō. Hoeru. To roar (as a lion), pant.
哲 Tetsu. Monoshiru, satoi. To be wise, a philosopher, intelligent.	哺 Ho. Kurau, fukumu. To eat, hold in the mouth.	唇 Shin. Kuchibiru. The lips.	唐 Tō. Kara, morokoshi. Name of old Chinese dynasty, 618-913 A. D., China, foreign.	啄 Taku. Tsuibamu. To pick up food (as a bird.)

啓	售	唯	唱	唾
Kei.	Shū.	I.	Shō.	Da.
Mōsu, hiraku, oshieru.	Uru.	Tada, hitori, ukegau.	Tonaeru, izanau.	Tsubaki.
To say, open, instruct.	To sell.	Only, alone, to assent.	To say, recite, name, accompany.	Saliva.

問	啜	啻	啼	善
Mon.	Setsu.	Shi.	Tei.	Zen.
Tou, tomurau.	Susuru.	Tada, tsumabiraka.	Naku.	Yoshi.
To enquire, examine into, visit.	To sup, snuff.	Only, clear.	To cry (used of men and animals generally), weep.	Goodness, virtue, good, right.

喉	喊	喋	喘	喙
Kō.	Kan.	Chō.	Zen.	Kai.
Nondo.	Toki no koe.	Kuchigimashii.	Aegu.	Kuchibashi.
The throat.	A cry, call, war-cry.	Noisy, querulous.	To pant, be asthmatic.	The bill, beak.

喚	喜	喝	喞	喧
Kwan.	Ki.	Katsu.	Shoku.	Ken.
Yobu, yobawaru.	Yorokobu.	Ibau, shikaru.	Naku, kamabisushii.	Kamabisushii.
To call, cry out.	To rejoice.	To call out, scold, cheer.	To cry, noisy.	Noisy.

喩	喪	喫	喬	喇
Yu.	Sō.	Kitsu.	Kiō.	Ratsu.
Satosu, tatoe.	Mo, ushinau, horobu.	Kurau, kamu, nomu.	Takai.	Kotobahayai.
To instruct, announce officially, warn, an example, comparison.	Mourning, to lose, be destroyed.	To eat, chew, drink, smoke.	High.	Talking fast. (叭 Rappa, a bugle.)

單	嗤	嗅	嗔	嗚
Tan.	Shi.	Kiū.	Shin.	O.
Hitotsu, hitoe, katagata.	Warau, azakeru.	Kagu.	Ikaru.	Aa.
One, single, singular, one side.	To laugh, laugh at.	To smell.	To be angry.	An interjection expressive of sorrow.

嗜 +	嗟	嗣	嗽	嘆 ✕
Shi.	Sa.	Shi.	Sō.	Tan.
Tashimu.	Nageku, aa.	Tsugu.	Kuchi susugu.	Nageku.
To be fond of, love.	To grieve, mourn, an interjection.	To inherit, succeed, next.	To wash out the mouth, cough, expectorate.	To grieve, mourn. 歎

嘉 ✕	嗾	嘔 +	嗇	嘗 ✕
Ka.	Sō.	Ō.	Shoku.	Shō.
Yomi suru, yoi, yorokobu.	Keshikakeru.	Haku.	Oshimu, musaboru.	Nameru, katsute.
To regard as good, good, happy.	To set a dog on, instigate.	To vomit.	To grudge, covet.	To lick, previously.

鳴 +	嘯 ✕	嘸 +	嘲 ✕	嘶
Mei.	Shō.	Bu.	Chō.	Sei.
Naku, naru.	Usobuku.	Sazo, kotaeru.	Azakeru.	Inanaku.
To cry, call, sound, ring.	To roar (as a tiger), whistle.	Very, how much, truly, to answer.	To laugh at, make a fool of.	To neigh, cry.

噂 +	噎	噴 +	噤	器 ✕
Son.	Etsu.	Fun.	Kin.	Ki.
Uwasa.	Musebu.	Haku, fukidasu.	Kuchifusagu, tsugumu.	Utsuwa.
Gossip, rumour.	To choke.	To vomit out, blow out, spout out.	To shut the mouth, be silent.	A vessel, utensil.

噪	噫	嚇	嚏	嚮
Sō.	I.	Kaku.	Tei.	Kiō.
Sawagu.	Aa, nageku.	Odoru, ikaru.	Hanahiru, kusame.	Saki ni, mukau.
To be in commotion, tumultuous.	An interjection expressive of sorrow, to grieve.	To threaten, be angry.	To sneeze.	Before, the past, to face, opposite.

嚴 ✕	嚻 ✕	囀	囃 ✕	囋
Gen.	Gō.	Ten.	Sō.	Shō.
Kibishii, ogosoka.	Kamabisushii.	Saezuru.	Hayasu.	Kamabisushii.
Strict, severe, to frighten.	Noisy.	To twitter, chatter.	To play on musical instruments, praise.	Noisy, chattering.

嗊 Shoku, soku. *Tsukeru, yoseru, atsuraeru.* To apply, trust in, order.	嚼 Ketsu. *Kamu.* To bite, chew.				
口 (The 31st Radical) I. *Meguri, kakomi.* An enclosure.	囚 Shū. *Meshiudo, toraeru.* A prisoner, criminal, convict, to arrest.	四 Shi. *Yotsu.* Four.	回 Kwai, e. *Meguru, kaeru, somuku.* To revolve, repeat, return, disobey, a time, chapter.	因 In. *Yoru, chinami, yotte.* To depend on, in connection with, because of, a cause, basis.	
囮 Kwa. *Otori.* A decoy.	困 Kon. *Komaru, kiwamaru, tsukareru.* To be in distress, in extremities, tired.	囹 Rei. *Hitoya.* A prison.	固 Ko. *Katai, katameru, koru, motoyori.* Hard, firm, obstinate, from the first, of course.	囿 Yū. *Sono, kagiru.* A park, garden, to bound.	
圃 Ho. *Hatake, sono.* A field, vegetable garden.	圄 Gio, go. *Torawareru.* To detain, imprison.	圈 Ken. *Magemono, meguru.* A round wooden box, a pen, to surround, a circle, point.	國 Koku. *Kuni.* A country, State. 国	圍 I. *Kakoi, kakomu.* To surround, preserve, an inclosure.	
園 En. *Sono, misasagi.* A garden, an Imperial tomb.	圓 En. *Madoka, marui.* Round, a dollar or yen.	團 Dan. *Madoka, atsumaru.* Round, to assemble, a band, company.	圖 Zu, to. *Hakaru, egaku.* A picture, map, opportunity, to plan.	圜 En, kwan. *Meguru, madoka.* To go round, round.	
土 (The 32nd Radical) To, do. *Tsuchi.* Earth.	在 Zai. *Aru, imasu.* To be, dwell, the country, now.	圭 Kei. *Tama.* A precious stone, sceptre.	地 Chi, ji. *Tsuchi, tokoro.* The earth, land, place.	坂 Han. *Saka.* An acclivity, part, rions, to be piled up.	土

均 KIN. *Hitoshii, tairaka.* Alike, equal, level.	坊 HŌ, BŌ. *Tsutsumi, chimata.* A dike, cross roads.	坐 ZA. *Iru, suwaru, tsumi serareru, sozoro.* To be, sit, be set, involved in, be punished, involuntarily.	坑 KŌ. *Ana, hori.* A hole, pit.	坤 KON. *Tsuchi, hitsuji-saru no kata.* The earth, the S. W.
坪 HEI. *Tairaka, tsubo.* Level, a land measure of 36 sq. ft.	坦 TAN. *Hiroi, tairaka.* Broad, level.	垂 SUI. *Tareru, nannan to suru.* To drop down, hang down, about to.	垢 KŌ. *Aka.* Dirt, filth.	垣 EN. *Kaki.* A fence, wall.
型 KEI. *Igata.* A mould.	埃 AI. *Hokori.* Dust.	埋 MAI. *Uzumeru, kakusu.* To bury, fill up, hide.	城 JŌ. *Shiro, ki.* A castle.	埒 RETSU, RACHI. *Kaki, kishi.* A fence, wall, bank.
域 IKI. *Tokoro, sakai.* A place, limit, boundary.	埠 FU, HO. *Tsuka, hatoba.* A mound, a landing place, wharf, port.	淤 O. *Doro, nigoru.* Mud, to be muddy.	執 SHITSU, SHŪ. *Toru, kakawaru, toraeru.* To take, take hold of, manage, transact.	培 BAI. *Tsuchikau.* To tend the roots of grain, &c., manure.
基 KI. *Motoi, hajime.* Foundation, basis, origin, beginning.	堀 KUTSU. *Horu, hori, abaku.* To dig, carve, tattoo, dig open, a canal.	堂 DŌ. *Takadono.* A public hall, chamber, place of religious worship, mansion.	堅 KEN. *Katai, tsuyoi, korai.* Hard, firm, strong, strict.	堆 TAI. *Uzudakai.* Piled up in heaps.
堇 KIN. *Tsuchinebari, sunawe.* Sticky, sive clay, the frights.	堡 HO. *Kojiro.* A small castle, an embankment.	堤 TEI. *Tsutsumi.* A bank, dike.	堪 KAN. *Taeru.* To endure, be able.	報 HŌ. *Mukuyuru, mōsu.* An answer, communication, to recompense, report.

堰 EN. ki, fusegu. m, to keep off.	堵 TO, DO. Kaki. A fence, wall, tranquil.	堺 KAI. Sakai, kagiru. A border, frontier, boundary, to limit.	塊 KWAI. Tsuchikure. A clod of earth.
塩 EN. Shio. Salt.	塗 TO. Doro, nuru. Mud, mire, to besmear, paint, lacquer.	塚 CHŌ. Tsuka, haka. A mound, grave.	塞 SAI, SOKU. Sakai, fusagu, ōu, michiru, saeru. A limit, boundary, to stop up, cover, be full.
毀 KI. tsu, yaburu, au, soshiru. reak, destroy, injure, slander.	塵 JIN. Chiri, hokori. Dirt, dust, rubbish.	塾 JUKU. Ie. A school, school-room.	境 KIŌ. Sakai. A limit, boundary, region, condition.
塋 BO. ika, haka. ound, grave.	墜 TSUI. Ochiru. To fall down.	増 ZŌ. Masu, kuwaeru. To increase, add,	墨 BOKU. Sumi. Ink, blacking.
墳 FUN. a, tsutsumi. ound, grave, dike.	墾 KON. Arakibari. Breaking up new ground and preparing it for cultivation.	壁 HEKI. Kabe, kaki. A wall.	壅 YŌ. Fusagu, sasaeru. To stop up, obstruct.
壑 GAKU. ani, hori. alley, ravine.	壓 ATSU. Fusagu, osu. To stop up, press down, oppress.	壕 GŌ. Hori. A moat, ditch.	壘 RUI. Soko, kasanaru. A wall, rampart, fortifications, to be piled up.

壙	壞 †	疆	壤 ✕	
Kwō.	Kwai.	Kiō.	Jō.	
Tsukaana.	Kuzusu, yaburu.	Sakai, kagiri.	Koetsuchi, sakai, kuzusu, yabureru.	
A grave, vault, mine.	To break down, destroy, ruin.	A limit, boundary, region.	Fertile ground, a boundary, region, to go to ruin, perish.	

士 ✕	壬	壯 ✕	壺 ✕	壹 ✕
The 33rd Radical)	Jin.	Sō.	Ko.	Itsu, ichi.
Shi.	Mizunoe, ninau.	Sukoyaka, tsuyoi, sakan.	Tsubo.	Hitotsu, moppara.
Samurai, onoko, tsukasa. A two-sworded man, a samurai, a man, soldier, governor.	The 9th of the ten calendar signs, to carry.	Strong, vigorous, flourishing, in the pride of youth.	A jar, vessel.	One, entirely, chiefly.

壽 ✕				
Ju.				
Inochinagai, hisashii, kotobuki.				
Long life, old age.				

夊				
The 34th Radical)				
Shi.				
Okureru.				
To follow.				

夂	夏 ✕			
The 35th Radical)	Ka.			
Sui.	Natsu.			
Yasushi.				
To walk slowly.	Summer.			

夢 ナ Mu. *Yume, kurai.* A dream, dark.	夥 ナ Kwa. *Ōi, obitadashii.* Many, numerous, very, violent.			
大 ナ (The 37th Radical) Tai, Dai. .. *Ōi naru, hanahada.* Great, big, chief, very, superlative.	天 ナ Ten. *Ame, sora.* The sky, weather, nature, heaven.	太 ナ Tai. *Ōi naru, hanahada, futoi.* Large, great, very, thick.	夫 ナ Fu. *Onoko, otto, sore, kano, kana.* A man, husband, that, an interjection.	夭 ナ Yō. *Wakai, wakajini, nobiyaka.* Young, an early death, expanded.
央 ナ Ō. *Mannaka, nakaba.* The middle, centre.	失 ナ Shitsu. *Ushinau, ayamaru, ayamachi.* To lose, err, a mistake.	夷 ナ I. *Ebisu, tairaka, horobosu.* A barbarian, level, to destroy.	尖 ナ Sen. *Togaru.* To be pointed, sharp.	夾 ナ Kyō. *Sashihasamu, chikai.* To hold on both sides, to place between two other things, near.
奇 ナ Ki. *Ayashii, katagata, amaru.* Strange, wonderful, odd (in numbers), to exceed, be left over.	奈 ナ Dai, Nai. *Ikan, nanzo.* How, what, why.	奉 ナ Hō. *Uketamawaru, tatematsuru.* To present to or receive from (a superior), perform official duties.	奏 ナ Sō. *Susumeru, kanaderu.* To report to or memorialize (the Emperor), to play on a musical instrument.	契 ナ Kei. *Warifu, chigiru.* A tally, to make an agreement or alliance with.
奔 ナ Hon. *Washiru.* To run.	奕 ナ Eki. *Ōi naru.* Great, large, to gamble.	套 ナ Tō. *Nagai.* Long.	奠 ナ Ten. *Sadameru, matsuru, oku.* To decide, worship, place.	奚 ナ Kei. *Nanzo.* How, why.
奢 ナ Sha. *Ogoru.* To be extravagant, profuse.	奥 ナ Ō, Oku. *Uchi, fukai.* Inside, the back, deep, a wife.	奪 ナ Datsu. *Toru, ubau.* To seize, take by force.	奬 ナ Shō. *Susumeru, tasukeru.* To exhort, encourage, assist.	奮 ナ Fun. *Furū, agaru.* To be stirred up, excited, enthusiastic.

女

女	奴	奸	好	妁
(The 38th Radical) Jo, Nio. Onna, me, musume. A woman, female, girl, daughter.	Do, Nu. Yakko. A servant, slave.	Kan. Okasu, midareru, katamashii, itsuwaru. To transgress, depraved, disorderly, adultery, to lie.	Kō. Uruwashii, yoi, yomisuru, konomu, yoshimi. Beautiful, good, to prize, love, friendship.	Shaku. Nakadachi. A go-between.
如 Jo, Nio. Gotoku, shiku, moshi, yuku. Like, as good as, if, to go.	妃 Hi. Kisaki. An Imperial concubine.	妄 Bō, Mō. Midari ni, itsuwaru. Improperly, disorderly, to lie.	妊 Nin. Haramu. To be with child.	妒 To. Netamu, sonemu. To envy, be jealous of.
妖 Yō. Tsuyayaka, ayashii, wazawai. Beautiful, strange, bewitching, supernatural, calamity.	妙 Miō. Taenaru, kasuka, wakai. Wonderful, admirable, young.	妥 Ta. Yasui, odayaka. Quiet, peaceful.	妓 Gi. Asobime. A singing-girl, prostitute.	妨 Bō. Samatage, yaburu Hindrance, injury, objection, to disturb, destroy.
妹 Mai. Imōto. A younger sister.	妻 Sai. Tsuma. A wife.	妾 Shō. Mekake, warawa. A concubine, I (used by women).	姆 Bō. Kashizuku. A governess, nurse, attendant.	姉 Shi. Ane. An elder sister.
始 Shi. Hajime. A beginning.	姑 Ko. Shūtome, oba, shibaraku. A mother-in-law, aunt, a short time, some time.	姓 Sei. Uji. A family or clan surname.	委 I. Yudaneru, makaseru, kuwashii. To entrust, commit, delegate, minute.	姣 Kō. Kaoyoi, kobiru. Good-looking, to flatter.
姥 Bo. Uba. An old woman.	姦 Kan. Okasu, midareru, katamashii, itsuwaru. To transgress, depraved, disorderly, adultery, to lie.	姪 Tetsu. Mei. A niece.	姫 Ki. Hime. A princess, queen, Imperial concubine.	姻 In. Totsugu, shūto. To marry (a husband) a father-in-law.

姿	威	娉	媲	孃
Shi.	I.	Hei.	Bi.	Jō.
Sugata.	Ogosoka, takei, odosu.	Metoru.	Utsukushii, shitagau.	Musume.
Form, appearance, manner.	Stern, majestic, fierce, strong, to threaten.	To marry (a wife).	Beautiful, to obey.	A girl, female.
娠	娛	娩	婢	娥
Shin.	Go.	Ben.	Hi.	Ga.
Haramu.	Tanoshimu.	Ko-umu.	Onnashimobe, koshimoto.	Mimeyoi.
To be pregnant.	To rejoice.	To beget a child.	A maid-servant.	Beautiful.
娶	娼	婦	婆	婚
Shu, sho.	Shō.	Fu.	Ha, ba.	Kon.
Metoru.	Tawamureru.	Yome, me.	Uba.	Yomeiri, yometori.
To marry (a wife).	To sport, a singing girl, prostitute.	A wife, woman.	An old woman, mother.	Marriage.
婉	婬	婿	媒	媚
En.	In.	Sei.	Bai.	Bi.
Kobiru, shitagau.	Tanoshimu, katamashii, yokoshima.	Muko.	Nakadachi, hakaru.	Kobiru.
To flatter, graceful, docile.	To rejoice (in a bad sense), depraved, evil, lewd.	A son-in-law.	A go-between, to consult.	To flatter.
媳	媼	媾	嫁	嫂
Seki.	Ō.	Kō.	Ka.	Sō.
Yome, hanayome.	Uba.	Au, itsukushimu, yawarageru.	Totsugu.	Aniyome.
A son's wife, wife, bride.	An old woman.	To meet, love, tranquillize, make peace.	To marry (a husband).	A sister in law, elder brother's wife.
嫉	嫌	嫩	嬌	嫡
Shitsu.	Ken.	Don, zen.	Kiō.	Teki, chaku.
Sonemu, nikumu.	Kirau, utagau, akitarazu.	Kaoyoi, wakai.	Kobiru.	Tadashii, kimi.
To envy, be jealous of, hate.	To hate, suspect, unsatisfied.	Good looking, young, tender.	To flatter.	The principal wife, direct, an heir.

嬋	嬖	嬪	嬰	嬾
Sen.	Hei.	Hin.	Ei.	Ran.
Taoyaka.	*Itsukushimu, sobazukae.*	*Hime.*	*Midorigo, kazari.*	*Okotaru, monoui.*
Graceful, tender.	To love, an attendant, favourite, concubine.	An Imperial concubine, a maid of honour.	A baby, an ornament.	To be negligent, lazy, averse to.
孀	孃			
Sō.	Jō.			
Yamome.	*Musume, haha.*			
A widow.	A female, girl, mother.			
子	孑	孔	孕	字
(The 39th Radical) Shi.	Ketsu.	Kō.	Yō.	Ji.
Ko, musuko, nanji, jū ni shi no ne.	*Nokoru, mijikai, bōfuriunshi, hitoe.*	*Yoi, hanahada, ana.*	*Haramu.*	*Moji, azana, yashinau.*
A child, boy, son, you, he "rat" (the 1st of the twelve horary characters), viscount.	To be left over, small, animalculæ, larva, alone.	Good, very, a hole, sage.	To be pregnant.	A character, the name commonly used, to nourish.
存	孚	孛	孜	孝
Son, zon.	Fu.	Hai.	Shi.	Kō.
Nagaraeru.	*Makoto, tamago wo kaesu.*	*Hōki boshi.*	*Tsutomeru, hagemu.*	*Tsukaeru, yashinau.*
To continue in life, remain, think, know.	Truth, to hatch an egg.	A comet.	To exert one's self, labour diligently.	Filial piety, to nourish.
孟	孤	季	孥	孩
Mō.	Ko.	Ki.	Do.	Gai.
Hajime, tsutomeru.	*Minashigo, hitori.*	*Wakai, sue.*	*Tsumako.*	*Osanago.*
The beginning, great, to exert one's self.	An orphan, alone.	Young, the end, a season.	Wife and child.	An infant.
孫	孰	孵	孳	學
Son.	Juku.	Fu.	Ji.	Gaku.
Mago.	*Tare, izure.*	*Yashinau, kaesu.*	*Umu, tsurumu, tsutomeru.*	*Narau, manabu, satoru, oboeru.*
A grandchild.	Who? what? where?	To nourish, hatch.	To bear young, copulate, exert one's self.	To learn, practise, study know, a place of learning.

(39)

孼 KETSU. no ko, sobame ko, wazawai. youngest child, an legitimate child, misfortune.			
宅 TAKU. Ie, idokoro. house, dwelling.	宇 U. Yomo, noki, ōi naru. The four Quarters of the Compass, the world, vast.	守 SHU. Mamoru, kami. To keep, guard, a Governor.	安 AN. Yasui, tanoshimu, izukunzo. Ease, tranquillity, happiness, where?
宏 KWŌ. naru, hiroi. eat, large, wide.	宕 TŌ. Hora-ana. A cave, covered way.	宗 SŌ, SHŪ. Tattobu, minamoto. To honour, the origin, fountain, head, sect.	官 KWAN. Tsukasa, ōyake. A government office, an official, pertaining to the government, public.
定 TEI, JŌ. Sadameru. to fix, establish.	宛 EN. Ōu, adakamo, zutsu, ate. To cover, just, exactly, each, addressed to.	宜 GI. Yoroshii, beshi, mube, ube. Good, right, proper, ought, should.	客 KAKU, KIAKU. Maroto, tabibito. A guest, stranger, visitor.
室 SHITSU. muro, tsuma. use, room, cellar, wife.	宥 YŪ. Yurusu, nadameru. To pardon, mitigate (a punishment).	宸 SHIN. Fukai ie. An Imperial Palace, Imperial.	宮 KIŪ, KU. Miya. A Shinto temple, Imperial Household, an Imperial Prince or Princess, Imperial.
害 GAI. onau, yaburu, wazawai. Injure, damage, calamity.	宴 EN. Sakamori, ikou, yasui. A banquet, to rest, quiet.	宵 SHŌ. Yoru, yoi. Night, evening.	家 KA, KE. Ie. A house, family.

容 ｲ	宿 ｲ	寂 ｲ	寄 ｲ	寅 ｲ
Yō.	Shuku.	Seki, Jaku.	Ki.	In.
Katachi, sugiru. Form, to have appearance, mild, bear, put up with, consent to.	Yadoru, yado, todomaru, mukashi. To stop, lodge, a lodging-place, post-station, olden times.	Sabishii, shizuka. Lonely, quiet, to die (of a Buddhist priest).	Yoru, yoseru, tsutaeru. To call at in passing, lodge, depend on, trust in, hand on, collect.	Tora, tsutsushimu. The "tiger," the 3rd of the twelve horary characters, to be respectful.
密 ｲ	寇 ｲ	富 ｲ	寐 ｲ	寒 ｲ
Mitsu.	Kō.	Fu, Fū.	Bi, Mi.	Kan.
Hisoka, shizuka. Secret, quiet, close, dense.	Ada, sokonau, kasumeru. An enemy, to injure, rob.	Tomi, saiwai. Wealth, riches, prosperity, a kind of lottery.	Neru, yasumu. To sleep, rest.	Samui, kogoeru. Cold, to freeze.
寓 ｲ	寔 ｲ	寖 ｲ	寞 ｲ	察 ｲ
Gū.	Shoku, Jiki.	Shin.	Baku.	Satsu.
Yoru, yadoru. To stop, lodge, sojourn.	Tada, makoto, kore. Only, truth, this.	Yaya. Gradually.	Sabishii, shizuka. Lonely, quiet.	Shiraberu, shiru, kangaeru, isagiyoi. To examine, know, reflect, pure.
寡 ｲ	寝 ｲ	寤 ｲ	寥 ｲ	實 ｲ
Kwa.	Shin.	Go.	Riō.	Jitsu.
Sukunai, yamome, hitori. Few, a widow, alone.	Neya, neru. A bed-room, to sleep.	Sameru, satoru. To awake, know.	Samushii, munashii. Lonely, empty.	Mi, michiru, makoto. Fruit, seed, to be full, true, real, sincere, kind.
寧 ｲ	寨 ｲ	審 ｲ	寫 ｲ	寬 ｲ
Nei.	Sai.	Shin.	Sha.	Kwan.
Mushiro, yasui. Rather, easy.	Toride. A fort, stronghold.	Kotogotoku, tsumabiraka, kiwameru. Altogether, particulars, evident, to decide, investigate thoroughly.	Utsusu. To copy, draw, photograph.	Yuruyaka, hiroi. Not strict, easy, gentle, wide, liberal, merciful.

寺 ギ	封 ギ	射 ギ	將 ギ	寸
Ji.	Hō, Fū.	Sha.	Shō.	
Tera.	*Tsutsumu, sakai, ōi naru.*	*Iru.*	*Hatamata, masa ni sakan, okonau.*	
Buddhist temple.	A boundary, fief, domain, to close up, seal, set over (as ruler), great.	To shoot, to dart (as light).	Moreover, just about, flourishing, to conduct, assist.	
尉 ギ	尊 ギ	尋 ギ	對 ギ	
I.	Son.	Jin.	Tai, tsui.	
Ilinoshi, yasunjiru.	*Tattobu, tattoi, mikoto.*	*Tazuneru, hiro.*	*Kotaeru, mukaiau.*	
Military title applied officers from the rank captain downwards, to calm.	To honour, honourable, you, a respectful title affixed to the name of a god or hero.	To enquire into, investigate, seek, a fathom.	To answer, correspond, confront, a pair.	
少 ギ	尚 ギ	鈔 ギ		小
Shō.	Shō.	Sen.		
ukunai, wakai.	*Kuwaeru, nao, tattobu.*	*Sukunai.*		
ew, little, young.	To add, still more, to reverence.	Few.		
尤 ギ	尨 ギ	就 ギ		尢
Yū.	Bō, mō.	Shū.		
tomo, togameru, imachi, ayashii.	*Mukuinu.*	*Tsuku, owari, naru.*		
ry, right, however, blame, a mistake, strange.	A shaggy dog.	To follow, belong to, relate to, the end, to become, finish.		
尺 ギ	尻 ギ	尼 ギ	尾 ギ	尸
Seki, shaku.	Kō.	Ni, ji.	Bi, mi.	
—	*Shiri, izarai.*	*Ama, todomeru.*	*O, sue, owari.*	
Japanese foot of ten inches.	The buttocks.	A Buddhist nun, to stop.	A tail, the end.	

尸	局 ✝	居 ✗	届 ✗	屈 ✗
Nīō, jō.	Kioku.	Kio.	Kai.	Kutsu.
Ibari.	Tsubone, kagamaru.	Oru, iru, suwaru, sueru, todomaru.	Itaru, todokeru, todoku.	Kagameru, magaru.
Urine.	A room, Government Bureau, office, woman's apartment, checker board, to bend.	To be, dwell, sit down, place, lay, stop.	To reach, arrive, be efficacious, forward, report, petition.	To bend, crooked, exhausted.
屋 ✗	屍	屎	屏 ✗	屐
Oku.	Shi.	Shi, ki.	Hei, biō.	Geki.
Ya, ie, todomaru.	Shikabane.	Kuso.	Ōu, shirizokeru.	Ashida.
A house, to stop.	A corpse.	Dung, filth.	To cover, send away, a screen.	Wooden shoes.
屑 ✗	展 ✗	屠 ✗	屢 ✗	層 ✗
Setsu.	Ten.	To.	Ru.	Sō.
Isagiyoi, kuzu.	Noberu, miru, tsuranaru.	Hofuru, korosu.	Shibashiba.	Shina, kasa, kasaneru.
Pure, rubbish, scraps.	To spread out, open, exhibit, look at, be arranged in a row.	To slaughter, kill.	Often.	A step, degree, heap, to pile up, still more.
履	屬 ✗			
Ri.	Shoku, zoku.			
Fumu, kutsu.	Tsuku, tsuzuku, tsuranaru, shinobu, sakiwan, tomogara.			
To tread on, perform, boots, shoes.	To belong to, attached to, subject to, arranged in a row, a servant, companion, an official appointed by the head of a department.			

屮

屮	屯 ✗			
(The 45th Radical)				
Tetsu.	Ton.			
Kusa hae izuru.	Tamuro, atsumaru.			
A plant sprouting.	An encampment, barracks, to assemble.			

山

山	屹 ✗	岐 ✗	岑 ✗	岡 ✗
(The 46th Radical)	Kitsu.	Ki.	Shin.	Kō.
San, sen.	Kewashii, sobadatsu.	Chimata, futamata.	Takai, mine.	Oka, yama no se.
Yama.				
A hill, mountain.	Steep, to tower up.	Forks in a road, to diverge, high.	High, a mountain peak.	A hill, a mountain ridge.

岨	岩 ✕	岬 ✕	岸 ✕	峙
Sho, so.	Gan.	Kō.	Gan.	Ji.
Tsuchiyama, kewashii.	Iwao, sagashii.	Yama no soba, misaki, kewashii.	Kishi.	Sobadatsu.
A hill, steep, a precipice.	A high bank, rocky cliff, hazardous.	The side of a hill, a cape.	A bank, cliff, shore.	To be lofty, tower up.
峠 ✕	峨	峯	峻	峽 ✕
—	Ga.	Hō, bō.	Shun.	Kiō.
Tōge.	Sagashii.	Mine. 峰	Kewashii, sagashii.	Soba, yama-ai.
A mountain pass, ascent, climax.	Steep, high.	A mountain peak.	Steep, precipitous.	A cliff, chasm, mountain gorge, strait.
崇	崎 ✕	崛	崕 ✕	崩 ✕
Shū, sō.	Ki.	Kutsu.	Gai.	Hō, bō.
Takai, tattobu, agameru.	Saki, misaki, sagashii.	Takai, tatsu.	Gake, kishi. 崖	Kuzureru.
High, to honour, exalt, adore.	A cape, promontory, steep.	High, to stand up.	A precipice, cliff.	To fall to pieces, die (used of the Emperor).
嵐 ✕	嵒	嵬	嵯	島 ✕
Ran.	Gan.	Kwai.	Sa.	Tō.
Arashi.	Iwao, sagashii.	Takai, kewashii.	Kewashii, sagashii.	Shima. 嶋
A storm.	A rock, rocky cliff, precipitous.	High, steep.	Steep, precipitous.	An island.
嶮	嶺 ✕	嶼	嶽 ✕	巒
Ken.	Rei, riō.	Sho.	Gaku.	Ran.
kewashii, sagashii.	Mine.	Shima.	Take. 岳	Mine.
Steep, precipitous.	A mountain peak.	A small island.	A lofty peak.	A mountain peak.
巓 ✕	巖 ✕			
Ten.	Gan.			
Itadaki.	Iwa, kishi, kewashii.			
The summit of a mountain.	A rock, cliff, steep, precipitous.			

工	工 ヌ	左 ヌ	巧 ヌ	巨 ヌ	巫 ヌ
	(The 48th Radical) Kō, KU. Takumi, tsukasa. Art, work, skill, craft, an artizan, workman, superintendent, officer.	SA. Hidari, tasukeru. The left, to assist.	Kō. Takumi, shiwaza. Meritorious actions, skill, talent, ingenuity, to devise, invent.	Kiō. Ōi naru. Great, large.	Fu. Kannagi, miko. A female dancer in a miya who pretends to have communication with the gods, a fortune-teller, witch.
	差 ヌ SA, SHI. Tagau, shina, nimi. To differ, difference, error.				
己	己 ヌ (The 49th Radical) KI, KO. Onore, mi, tsuchinoto. A personal pronoun, one's self, the 6th of the ten calendar signs.	已 ヌ I. Yamu, owaru, sudeni, nomi. To stop, end, already, only.	巳 ヌ SHI. Mi. The "snake," the 6th of the twelve horary characters.	巴 ヌ HA. Tomoe. A comma shaped figure, a sign.	危 ヌ KI. Ayaui. Dangerous.
	巷 ヌ Kō. Chimata. A fork in a by-street, road, the town, common people.	巽 ヌ SON. Tatsumi, yuwaraka. The South East, the part of the day from 8 to 10 a. m., soft.			
巾	巾 ヌ (The 50th Radical) KIN. Haba, tenugui, fukusa. A napkin, headgear, a handkerchief, a cover.	凧 ヌ — Tako. A kite.	布 ヌ Fu. Nuno, shiku. Linen, cotton cloth, grass cloth, to spread, publish, make	帆 ヌ HAN. Ho. A sail.	希 ヌ KI. Mare, koinegau. Rare, to request or desire earnestly.

帑 Do. Kanegura. A treasury, safe.	帖 ✗ Chō. Shirusu, tarenuno, fuda. To write down, a curtain, ticket, document.	帙 ✗ Chitsu. Fumizutsumi. A cover or case for books, a classifier of letters.	帛 ✗ Haku. Kinu, mitegura. White silk, a present or offering of silk.	帝 ✗ Tei. Kimi, mikado. A Sovereign, Emperor.
帥 ✗ Sui. Hikiyuru, tsukasa, suberu. To lead, rule, control.	師 ✗ Shi. Tsukasa, moromoro, nori. A teacher, ruler, a model, expert, a brigade, the people.	席 ✗ Seki. Shikimono, mushiro. A mat, seat, assembly, room, place of meeting.	帳 ✗ Chō. Tobari, tarenuno. A register, account book, ledger, curtain, tent.	帶 ✗ Tai. Obi, obiru. A girdle, to wear, have.
帷 I. Katabira, tobari, maku. A summer garment of hemp, curtain, tent.	常 ✗ Jō. Tsune. Usual, ordinary, fixed.	帽 ✗ Bō. Kashirazutsumi. A hat.	幄 ✗ Aku. Maku. A curtain, tent.	幅 ✗ Fuku. Haba, mukabaki. Breadth, leggings, a hanging picture, numeral for hanging pictures.
幕 ✗ Maku, baku. Ōu. A curtain, tent, to cover, the Shogunate.	幡 ✗ Han. Hatajirushi, fukin. A flag, napkin.	幣 ✗ Hei. Nusa, mitegura, takara. The cut paper or silk hung in a miya to represent, or as an offering to, the kami, coin, money, wealth.	幬 ✗ Chū. Taremono, kaya. A curtain, mosquito net.	
干 ✗ The 51th Radical) Kan. Tate, okasu, migiwa, hiru, azukaru. A shield, to oppose, protect, the bank of a river, to dry, ebb, meddle with.	平 ✗ Hei, Hiō. Taira, tairageru. Level, equal, even, to quell, quiet.	年 ✗ Nen. Toshi, minoru. A year, to ripen.	幷 ✗ Hei, Hiō. Narabu, narabini, tomoni, awaseru. To be arranged in a row, together, with, unitedly, and, also.	幸 ✗ Kō. Saiwai, negau, miyuki. Happiness, luck, to ask for, going out or travelling (of the Emperor).
幹 ✗ Kan. Miki, kuki, tsuyoi. A trunk, stalk, strong, to manage.				

(46)

玄	幻 ✕	幼 ✕	幽 ✕	幾 ✕
(The 52th Radical) Yō. Wakai, itokenai. Young, small, tender.	GEN. Maboroshi, madowasu. An optical illusion, magic, sleight of hand.	Yō. Wakai, itokenai, osanai. Young.	Yū. Kurai, kasuka, kakureru, torawareru. Dark, to hide, be dim, imprisoned.	KI. Sukunai, kizashi, hotondo, chikai, iku. Few, the unseen beginning of things, near, how many.
广 (The 53th Radical) GEN, KAN. Ieaya, muneyi. A shelter, covering.	庀 ✕ HI. Hisashi, ōu. A shelter, pent-house, to cover.	床 ✕ SHŌ. Yuka, toko. The floor, boards, a bed, couch.	序 ✕ JO. Tsuide, tsuizuru, noberu. Order, arrangement, opportunity, to arrange in order, the preface (of a book).	底 ✕ TEI. Soko, itaru, todokōru. The bottom, to reach, be obstructed.
庖 HŌ. Kuriya. A kitchen.	店 ✕ TEN. Mise, tana. A shop.	庚 ✕ KŌ. Kanoe, kawaru. The 7th of the ten calendar signs, to change, age.	府 ✕ FU. Kura, miyako. A storehouse, city, capital, Government Department.	庠 ✕ SHŌ. Monomanabidokoro tsumabiraka ni suru. A school, to make clear.
度 ✕ DO, TAKU. Nori, nottoru, wataru, hakaru. A rule, to imitate, crosses over, measure, a degree of latitude or time, a consecrative suffix.	庫 ✕ KO. Kura, bukigura. A godown, military storehouse.	座 ✕ ZA. Idokoro, kurai. A seat, assembly, position.	庭 ✕ TEI. Niwa, tairaka. A garden, courtyard, site, level.	庵 ✕ AN. Iori, marui ie. A cottage, round house, small religious building.
庶 ✕ SHO. Moromoro, negau. All, numerous, the people, to request, a mistress.	庸 ✕ YŌ. Mochiiru, yetou, tsune. To use, employ, ordinary.	康 ✕ KŌ. Yasui, shizuka. Easy, peaceful.	廉 ✕ REN. Kiyoi, isagiyoi, kado. Pure, an item, article.	廊 ✕ RŌ. Hosodono, watari-dono. A corridor, porch, gallery, chamber.
廐 ✕ KIŪ. Umaya. A stable.	廓 ✕ KWAKU. Hiraku, munashii, ōi naru. To open, empty, large, an enclosure.	廚 ✕ CHU. Kuriya. A kitchen.	廛 ✕ TEN. Ichigura, mise. A shop, warehouse, market.	廝 ✕ SHI. Umakai, tsukawarebito. A groom, servant.

廟	廠	廡	廢	廣
Biō.	Snō.	Bu.	Hai.	Kwō.
Yashiro, tamaya.	Umaya, enshōgura.	Noki, hisashi.	Shirizoku, sutaru, yamu.	Hiroi.
A tomb, an ancestral temple, Government.	A shed, storehouse, magazine.	Eaves, a vestibule.	To withdraw, throw away, abolish, cease.	Vide.

廩	廬	廳		
Rin.	Ro.	Chō.		
Kura, yonegura.	Iori.	Ie, matsurigotodokoro.		
A godown, granary.	A cottage.	A building, Government Office.		

廴	延	廷	建	廻
(The 54th Radical)	En.	Thi.	Ken.	Kwai.
In. Hiku.	Noliru, hiku, oyobosu.	Niwa, tairaka.	Tateru.	Meguru.
To draw.	To extend, postpone, prolong.	The Imperial Court, a court, level.	To build, raise, establish.	To go round.

廾	廿	弄	弊	
(The 55th Radical)	Jū, niū.	Rō.	Hei.	
Kiū. Awaseru.	Hatachi.	Moteasobu, tawamureru.	Yaburu, ashii, kurushimu, kuse.	
To join or fold hands (as when presenting anything).	Twenty.	To play with.	Vile, abject, mean, bad, bad habits, torn, in distress, my (used in a depreciatory sense).	

弋	式	弑		
The 56th Radical)	Shiki, shoku.	Shi.		
Yoku. Igurumi.	Nori.	Korosu.		
An arrow with cord attached, to let fly an arrow.	Law, rule, custom, ceremony.	To kill a parent, master, or other superior, murder.		

弓	弔	引	弗	弘
(The 57th Radical)	Chō.	In.	Futsu.	Kō.
Kiū. Yumi.	Tomurau, awaremu, tsurusu.	Hiku.	Arazu, nashi, zu.	Ōinaru, hiromeru.
A bow.	To lament for, condole with, hang.	To draw, conduct, cite, quote.	Not so, not, dollar sign.	Great, large, to publish, promulgate, advertise.

(48)

弛	弦	弟 ナ	弱 ナ	張 ナ
SHI.	GEN.	TEI, DAI.	JAKU.	CHŌ.
Yurumeru, hazusu.	*Yumizuru.*	*Otōto.*	*Yowai, osanai.*	*Haru, ōinaru.*
To loosen, unfasten, relax.	A bow-string, chord.	A younger brother, junior.	Weak, young, a little less than the exact amount.	To stretch, spread, publish, boast, large, great.
強 ナ	彈 ナ	彌 ナ	彎 ナ	
KIŌ, GŌ.	TAN, DAN.	BI.	WAN.	
Tsuyoi, shiiru, anayachi ni.	*Hajiku, tadasu.*	*Iyoiyo, habikoru.*	*Hiku, magaru, soru.*	
Strong, violent, to force, urge, regardless of right.	To jerk, a spring, bullet, pill, to correct, act as censor.	Still more, to spread out, complete.	To draw, bend, arched.	
ヨ The 58th Radical) KEI. *Inokashira.* A pig's head, hog with snout upturned.	彗 SEI, SUI. *Hōkiboshi, akiraka.* A comet, clear.	彙 ナ I. *Tagui.* A sort, kind, to classify, collect.		
彡 The 59th Radical) SAN, SEN. *Ke no kazari.* Ornaments for the hair, feathers.	形 ナ KEI, GIŌ. *Katachi, arawareru.* Figure, shape, appearance, to be manifest.	彦 ナ GEN. *Sugureru, hiko.* Excellent, an honourable title applied to a deity or man.	彩 ナ SAI. *Iro-doru.* To colour, paint.	彫 ナ CHŌ. *Chiribameru, eru, kizamu, horu.* To engrave, carve, tattoo.
彰 ナ SHŌ. *Akiraka, arawareru, aya.* Clear, to be manifest, ornamented with figures, variegated.	影 ナ EI. *Kage, hibiki.* Shade, shadow, echo, image.			
彳 The 60th Radical) TEKI. *Tatazumu.* To stop, stand still, step short.	彷 ナ HŌ. *Tatazumu, tachi-y'suruu.* To stop, go to and fro, hesitate.	彼 ナ HI. *Kare, kano, koshiko.* That, he, she, it, they, there.	役 ナ YAKU, EKI. *Tsukau.* To employ, office, duty, service, government employment, a campaign, war-time.	往 ナ Ō. *Yuku, inishie, saki.* To go, the past, formerly.

征 ㄔ	徊 ㄔ	待 ㄔ	律 ㄔ	後 ㄔ
SEI.	KWAI.	TAI.	RITSU.	GO, KŌ.
Yuku, tadasu, toru, utsu.	Tachiyasurau.	Matsu, aishirau.	Tadasu, nori.	Nochi, ato, osoi, okureru.
To go, correct, take, reduce to submission.	To go to and fro, hover about.	To wait for, entertain.	To enquire into, a law, statute.	After, behind, late, next, future.

徐 ㄔ	徑 ㄔ	徒 ㄔ	得 ㄔ	徘 ㄔ
JO.	KEI.	TO.	TOKU.	HAI.
Omomuro ni.	Wataru, komichi, chikamichi.	Itazura ni, tomogara, yakko, kachi, tada.	Eru, uru.	Tachiyasurau.
Gently, leisurely.	To pass along, a by-path, short cut.	In vain, followers, servants, on foot, transportation, only.	To get, gain, profit, success, able.	To go to and fro.

從 ㄔ	御 ㄔ	徧 ㄔ	徨 ㄔ	復 ㄔ
JŪ.	GIO, GO.	HEN.	KWŌ.	FUKU.
Shitagau, tomo wo suru, yori.	Suberu, hamberu, tsukau, o, on, mi.	Amaneku. 遍	Tatazumu, honoka.	Kaeru, kaesu, mōsu, mata, kasaneru.
To follow, obey, accompany, from.	To follow, obey, drive (horses), attend on, Imperial, used as an honorific.	The whole, everywhere.	To stop, go to and fro, indistinct.	To return, report, restore, repeat, again.

循 ㄔ	微 ㄔ	徵 ㄔ	德 ㄔ	徹 ㄔ
JUN.	BI.	CHŌ.	TOKU.	TETSU.
Shitagau, meguru.	Kasuka, chiisai, iyashii.	Mesu, akiraka.	Megumu, saiwai, nori.	Tōru, itaru.
To follow, obey, revolve.	Dim, small, mean, humble.	To call, summon, clear, to levy, enlist.	Virtue, to be kind, happiness, doctrine.	To pervade, reach, penetrate.

徼	徽
KIŌ.	KI.
Motomeru, saegiru.	Nawa, mukabaki, yoi, shirushi.
To ask for, obtain, obstruct.	A cord, mark, emblem, leggings, good.

心 ㄔ	必 ㄔ	忌 ㄔ	忍 ㄔ	志 ㄔ	心 忄
(The 61st Radical) SHIN. Kokoro.	HITSU.	KI.	NIN.	SHI.	
The heart, mind.	Kanarazu.	Imi, imu, osoreru.	Shinobu, koraeru.	Kokorozashi, kokorozasu, shirusu.	
	Certainly, necessarily.	Mourning, to dislike, avoid, fear.	To bear with patience, endure.	Purpose, intention, to aim at, desire, write down.	

忘 ト	忙 ヶ	忝 ン	忠 ヶ	忤
Bō.	Bō.	Ten.	Chū.	Go.
Wasureru.	Isogashii.	Katajikenai, hazukashii.	Sunao, magokoro, mameyaka.	Sakau, motoru.
To forget.	Busy, hurried.	Thankful, much obliged, ashamed.	Fidelity, loyalty, patriotism.	To oppose

快 ト	念 ト	忸 ト	忻	忽 ヶ
Kwai.	Nen.	Chū.	Kin.	Kotsu.
Kokoroyoi, yorokobu.	Omou, tonaeru.	Narau, nareru.	Yorokobu.	Karonjiru, wasureru, yurukase, tachimachi.
Comfortable, happy, to rejoice.	To think of, recite, thought, care, attention, information.	To imitate, accustomed to.	To rejoice.	To make light of, forget, careless, immediately, suddenly.

忿	怱 ヶ	怏	怒 ト	怕 ヶ
Fun.	Sō.	Ō.	Do.	Ha, haku.
Ikaru.	Isogawashii.	Kokoroyokarazu, akitarazu.	Ikaru, ikidōru.	Osoreru.
To be angry.	Busy, hurried.	Uncomfortable, unhappy, gloomy, discontented.	To be angry.	To fear.

怖 ｲ	怙	怜	思 ヶ	怠 ヶ
Fu.	Ko.	Rei.	Shi.	Tai.
Osoreru.	Tanomu.	Satoi.	Omou.	Okotaru.
To fear.	To request, rely on.	Intelligent.	To think, reflect.	To be idle.

怡	急 ト	性 ト	怨 ヶ	怪 ト
I.	Kiū.	Sei, shō.	En.	Kwai.
Yorokobu, tanoshimu.	Isogu.	Umaretsuki.	Uramu.	Ayashii, ayashimu
To rejoice.	Urgent, express, to hasten.	Nature, natural quality, disposition.	To resent, hate.	Strange, wonderful, to be surprised at.

怯 ト	恟	恒 ト	恃 ト	恊 ヶ
Kiō.	Kiō.	Kō.	Ji.	Kiō.
Osoreru, ononoku.	Sawadatsu, osoreru.	Tsune, amaneku.	Tanomu.	Kanau, yawaragu.
To fear, tremble with fear.	Much excited, alarmed.	Usual, common, everywhere.	To request, rely on.	To agree with, be in harmony with.

恕 ✕ Jo. *Omoiyaru.* To excuse, bear patiently, judge of others by one's own feelings, sympathize with.	恗 ✕ Ko. *Ogoru, osoreru.* To be proud, fear.	恙 ✕ Yō. *Tsutsuga.* Harm.	恚 ✕ I. *Ikidōru, ikaru.* To be angry.
恣 Shi. *Ioshiimama ni.* An one pleases, in one's own way.	恤 ✕ Jutsu. *Megumu, nigiwasu.* To show kindness, to relieve.	恨 ✕ Kon. *Uramu.* To resent, hate.	恩 ✕ On. *Megumu, itsukushimu.* Favour, kindness, benefits.
息 ✕ Soku. *Iki, yasumu.* Breath, to rest.	恰 ✕ Gō. *Adakamo.* Just as, exactly.	悦 ✕ Etsu. *Yorokobu, tanoshimu.* To rejoice.	悉 ✕ Shitsu. *Kotogotoku, tsukusu.* All, to exhaust.
悋 Rin. *busaka, oshimu.* Miserly, to grudge.	悌 Tei. *Yasui.* Brotherly love, easy, amiable.	悍 Kan. *Isamu, takei, motoru.* Fierce, violent, to oppose.	悖 Hai. *Motoru, sakau.* To oppose.
悛 Sen, shun. *Aratameru, yameru.* To amend, stop.	悟 ✕ Go. *Satoru, satosu.* To know, perceive, instruct.	悠 ✕ Yū. *Haruka, hisashi.* Far off, a long time, anxious.	患 ✕ Kwan. *Ureōru.* To sorrow, be distressed.
悴 ✕ Sui. *ajikeru, ureōru.* To be cold, numb, sorrow.	悵 Chō. *Nageku, kanashimu.* To grieve.	悶 Mon. *Modaeru.* To feel pain or sorrow.	悼 ✕ Tō. *Itamu, kanashimu.* To grieve, be pained.

情 †	惆	惑 ☓	惕	惚
Jō.	Chū.	Waku.	Teki.	Kotsu.
Nasake, kokoro.	Modaeru, itamu.	Madou, madoi.	Osoreru, tsutsu-shimu.	Horeru, obomeku, uttori.
The feelings, kindness, pity, condition.	To feel pain or sorrow.	To err, be beguiled, delusion, superstition, doubt.	To fear, be respectful, circumspect.	To be bewitched, fall in love, be doubtful about, absent-mindedly.
惜 †	惟 †	忻	惠 †	惡 †
Seki.	I.	Kin.	Kei.	Aku, O.
Oshimu.	Omommiru, tada, hitori.	Yorokobu.	Megumi, itsuku-shimu.	Ashii, minikui, nikumu.
To grudge.	To reflect, only, alone.	To rejoice.	Kindness, favour, blessing, good will.	Bad, ugly, to hate.
惣 †	恬	惱 ☓	想 ☓	惴
Sō.	Da.	Nō.	Sō.	Zui.
Subete.	Okotaru.	Nayamu.	Omou, omoiyaru.	Osoreru.
All.	To be idle.	To be distressed, afflicted.	To think, imagine.	To fear, be sorrowful.
惶 ☓	惹 ☓	惻	愉	愁 ☓
Kwō.	Ja, nia, jaku.	Soku.	Yu.	Shū.
Awateru, osoreru, niwaka.	Hiku, midareru.	Itamashii, kuyashimu.	Kokoroyoi.	Urei, kanashimu.
To be excited, fear, sudden.	To provoke, attract, be confused.	Painful, to sorrow.	Comfortable, happy.	Sorrow.
愈 ☓	愆	愍	愎	意 ☓
Yu.	Ken.	Bin.	Fuku.	I.
Iyoiyo, ieru.	Ayamachi, toga.	Awaremu, kana-shimu.	Motoru, tagau.	Kokoro, kokoro-base.
More and more, still more, to be cured.	An error, fault.	To pity, sorrow.	To oppose.	The mind, will, meaning, feeling.
愕 †	愛 †	愚 ☓	感 ☓	慍
Gaku.	Ai.	Gu.	Kan.	Un.
Odoroku.	Itsukushimu, awaremu.	Oroka.	Ugoku, kotaeru.	Ikidōru, ikaru.
To be frightened.	Love, pity, tenderness.	Foolish.	To move, feel, admire.	To be angry.

愧	恕	愼	慨	慄
Kɪ.	So.	Shin.	Kɪ, kaɪ.	Ritsu.
Haji, hajiru.	*Uttaeru, tsugeru.*	*Tsutsushimu.*	*Tameiki, nageku, itaru.*	*Osoreru, ononoku.*
Shame, disgrace, to be ashamed.	To accuse, state, inform.	To be respectful, circumspect.	A long breath, sigh, to grieve, reach.	To fear, tremble with fear.
慇	慈	慊	態	慌
In.	Jɪ.	Ken.	Taɪ.	Kwō.
Nengoro.	*Itsukushimi.*	*Kokoroyoi.*	*Shiwaza, narifuri, wazato.*	*Honoka, kurai, osoreru.*
Courteous, earnest, kind.	Paternal or maternal love, charity, to love.	Comfortable, happy.	Work, appearance, manner, on purpose.	Dim, dark, to fear.
慕	慘	慙	慝	慟
Bo.	San, zan.	Zan.	Joku, toku.	Dō.
Shitau.	*Itamashii, mugoi.*	*Haji, hajiru.*	*Ashii, kakusu.*	*Nageku, naku.*
To love, long for.	Painful, cruel.	Shame, disgrace, to be ashamed. 慚	Bad, to hide.	To grieve, cry.
慢	慣	慥	慧	憂
Man.	Kwan.	Sō.	Keɪ.	Yū.
Anadoru, okotaru.	*Narau.*	*Tashika.*	*Satoi.*	*Urei, ureōru.*
To despise, be idle, lazy.	To be accustomed to, familiar with.	Certain.	Intelligent.	Grief, to sorrow, be anxious.
慨	慷	慮	愴	慰
Gaɪ.	Kō.	Rɪo.	Shō.	I.
Nageku, tameiki.	*Nageku, itamu.*	*Omompakaru.*	*Itamu, ureōru.*	*Nagusami.*
To grieve, a long breath, sigh.	To grieve, public-spirited.	To consider.	To grieve, sorrow.	Amusement, diversion, consolation.
慳	慴	慵	慶	慾
Ken.	Shō.	Shō.	Keɪ.	Yoku.
Oshimu.	*Ononoku, osoreru.*	*Monoui.*	*Yorokobu, iwau, saiwai.*	*Musaboru.*
To grudge.	To tremble with fear, fear.	Lazy, indolent.	To rejoice, congratulate, happiness.	Passion, lust, to covet.

(54)

憑	憎	憐	憫	憲
Hiō.	Zō.	Ren.	Bin.	Ken.
Yoru, tanomu.	Nikumu.	Awaremu.	Awaremu.	Nori.
To rely on, apply to.	To hate.	To pity.	To pity.	Law, ordinance, constitution.

憚	憩	憤	憮	憖
Tan.	Kei.	Fun.	Bu.	Gin.
Habakaru, osoreru.	Ikou.	Ikidōru, ikaru.	Kobiru, itamu.	Namajikka.
To fear.	To rest.	To be angry, indignant, zealous.	To flatter, grieve.	Hastily, without deliberation, right or wrong.

憶	憾	憨	懇	懈
Oku.	Kan.	Kin.	Kon.	Kai, ke.
Omou, shirusu.	Uramu.	Nengoro.	Nengoro.	Okotaru, monoui.
To think, note.	To resent, hate.	Courteous, earnest, zealous.	Courteous, earnest, zealous.	To be idle.

應	懟	懦	懲	懿
Ō.	Tai, tsui.	Da.	Chō.	I.
Kotaeru, ataru, masa ni.	Uramu, nikumu.	Yowai, okureru.	Korasu.	Yoi.
To agree with, correspond to, be proper, respond to, obey, accordingly.	To resent, hate.	Weak, to be late.	To punish, threaten, convict.	Good.

懶	懷	懸	懺	懼
Ran.	Kwai.	Ken.	Zan.	Ku.
Namakeru, monoui.	Idaku, futokoro, omou, nazukeru.	Kakaru.	Kuyuru.	Osoreru.
To be idle, negligent, averse to.	To embrace, the bosom, to think, tame, gain the friendship of.	To hang, concern, depend on, duty, cost, to be anxious.	To regret, repent.	To fear.

懽	戀			
Kwan.	Ren.			
Yorokobu.	Koiru, shitau.			
To rejoice.	To love, long after.			

欵

戈 (The 62nd Radical) KWA. *Hoko.* A spear, lance, javelin, war.	戊 Bō. *Tsuchinoe.* The fifth of the ten calendar signs.	戌 JUTSU. *Inu.* The "dog," the 11th of the twelve horary characters.	戍 JU. *Yadoru, mamoru.* To lodge, guard, protect the frontier.	戎 JŪ. *Tsuwamono, ebisu.* A soldier, barbarian, war.
成 JŌ, SEI. *Naru, owaru, nasu.* To become, finish, perform.	我 GA. *Ware, waga.* I, my, we, our.	戒 KAI. *Imashime, imashimeru.* Prohibition, commandment, to admonish, punish, warn.	戕 SHŌ. *Sokonau, korosu.* To injure, kill.	或 WAKU. *Aruiwa, moshikuwa.* Or, if, perhaps, doubtful.
戚 SEKI. *Shitashimu, ureiru.* To be friendly, intimate with, grieve, pity.	戟 GEKI. *Hoko.* A lance with two points, halberd.	戢 SHŪ. *Osameru, atsumeru.* To store up, collect.	戡 CHIN, KAN. *Katsu, kiru.* To conquer, kill, cut.	戮 RIKU. *Korosu, hazukashimeru, awaseru.* To kill, insult, unite.
戰 SEN. *Tatakau.* To fight, war, tremble with fear.	戲 GI, GE. *Tawamureru, moteasobu.* To play, sport.	戴 TAI, DAI. *Itadaku.* To put on the head, receive respectfully, sustain.		
戶 (The 63rd Radical) KO. *To.* A door, house, family.	戾 REI. *Motoru, modosu, itaru, yamu.* To oppose, return, reach, stop.	房 BŌ. *Ie, tsubone, fusa.* A house, room.	所 SHO. *Tokoro.* A place, that which, cause.	扁 HEN. *Fuda, hitotsu.* A tablet, one.
扇 SEN. *Ōgi, aogu.* A fan, to fan, winnow.	扉 HI. *Tobira, toboso.* A door, the hinge or leaf of a door, title page of a book.			

手	才	打	扛	扠
The 61th Radical) SHU. Te.	SAI.	DA.	KŌ.	SA.
	Hataraki, wazuka.	Utsu.	Ageru, ninau.	Sate.
The hand, arm, handle.	Ability, talent, few.	To beat, strike.	To raise, carry.	It being so (used to introduce a new subject).
扣	扞	扮	扱	扶
KŌ.	KAN.	FUN.	KIŪ.	FU.
Hikaeru, tataku.	Fusegu, mamoru.	Nigiru, ugoku, nazorau.	Toru, atsukau.	Tasukeru, tamotsu.
To refrain, withdraw, jot down, knock, appeal.	To ward off, defend.	To grasp, move, act the part of.	To manage, transact, take, deal with.	To assist, protect.
批	承	技	扗	拚
HI.	SHŌ.	GI.	KIŌ.	BEN.
Utsu, osu, shimesu.	Tsukamatsuru, ukeru, uketamawaru.	Waza, takumi.	Midareru, magete.	Te utsu.
To strike, push, show, publish, criticize.	To receive, acknowledge.	Art, skill, expertness.	To be confused, to perform an action against one's will.	To clap the hands.
抄	抉	把	抑	抗
SHŌ.	KETSU.	HA.	YOKU.	KŌ.
Kasumeru, utsusu, nuku.	Kujiru.	Toru, tsukamu.	Todomeru, osaeru, osumeru, somosomo.	Ageru, fusegu.
To rob, copy, extract, abstracts.	To pick, gouge out.	To take, hold.	To stop, restrain, govern, a particle used to introduce a new subject.	To raise, oppose, protest.
抓	抔	投	折	抴
SŌ.	HO, FU.	TŌ.	SHITSU.	EI, ETSU.
Kaku, tsumeru.	Nado, tsukamu.	Nageru, itaru.	Kujiku, oru, wakajini.	Hiku.
To scratch, pinch.	And so on, to take in both hands.	To throw, reach, send (as a letter).	To break, bend, fold, an early death.	To pull, draw.
披	抱	抵	抹	押
HI.	HŌ.	TEI.	MATSU.	KŌ, Ō.
Hiraku.	Idaku, kakaeru.	Ataru, fureru.	Nurikesu.	Shirusu, osu, osaeru.
To open.	To embrace, hold, engage.	To strike against, reach, resist.	To blot out, erase.	To mark, push, govern.

(57)

拂 ✗	拄	拆	拇
Futsu.	Chu.	Taku.	Bō.
Harau.	Sasaeru.	Hiraku, utsu.	Oyayubi.
o clear away, pay.	To obstruct, ward off, support.	To open, break open, destroy, strike.	The thumb.
拉	拊	抛	拍 ✗
Rō.	Fu.	Hō.	Haku, Hiō.
Torihishigu, kujiku.	Utsu, naderu.	Nageutsu, suteru.	Utsu.
o humble, destroy, hold down.	To strike, smooth.	To throw away.	To beat, strike.
拑	拒 ✗	拓 ✗	拔 ✗
Ken.	Kio.	Taku.	Batsu.
ameru, wakibasamu.	Fusegu, kobamu.	Hiraku.	Nuku.
o fit into, inlay, ld under the arm.	To ward off, reject.	To open, take up in the hand.	To pull out.
拙 ✗	招 ✗	拜 ✗	括
Setsu.	Shō.	Hai.	Kwatsu.
Tsutanai.	Maneku.	Ogamu.	Kukuru, musubu.
orant, I, my, (used 1 a depreciatory sense.)	To invite.	To worship, pray.	To tie, unite in one.
拱	拳	拴	拯
Kiō.	Ken.	Sen.	Shō.
Komanuku.	Kobushi, tsutsushimu.	Erabu.	Sukū, tasukeru.
o fold the hands.	The fist, to be respectful, circumspect.	To choose.	To scoop up, assist.
拶 ✗	拷	捐 ✗	拾 ✗
Satsu.	Gō.	En.	Shū, Jū.
Semaru.	Utsu.	Suteru, yudaneru.	Hirou, tō.
press upon, urge.	To strike, torture.	To throw away, give up, entrust, contribute.	To pick up, ten.

持	指	挈	按	挍
Ji.	Shi.	Ketsu, Kei.	An.	Kō.
Motsu, tamotsu.	Yubi, sasu.	Hissageru, ageru.	Kangaeru, osaeru.	Kangaeru, kuraberu.
To have, hold, keep.	A finger, to point.	To carry in the hand, raise.	To consider, repress.	To discuss, compare.
挑	挨	挫	振	挺
Chō.	Ai.	Za.	Shin.	Tei.
Idomu.	Osu, semaru.	Kujiku, torihishigu.	Furū.	Nuku.
To challenge, entice, defy.	To push, press upon, urge.	To break, sprain, dislocate, destroy.	To shake, quake, exercise, stir up.	To pull out, decided.
挽	挾	捉	捌	捍
Ban.	Kiō.	Soku.	Betsu.	Kan.
Hiku.	Sashihasamu.	Toraeru.	Sabaku, wakatsu.	Mamoru.
To lead.	To hold under the arm, hold, cherish.	To seize, arrest.	To unravel, judge, sell.	To ward off, defend.
捏	捕	捧	捨	捫
Detsu.	Ho.	Hō.	Sha.	Mon.
Koneru, hineru.	Toraeru.	Sasageru.	Suteru, hanatsu.	Toru, hineru.
To knead, mix.	To seize, arrest.	To present to a superior.	To throw away, let go.	To touch, twist, hold.
据	捲	捷	捺	捻
Kio.	Ken.	Shō.	Natsu.	Chō.
Sueru, agaku, kagamaru.	Maku, kakageru.	Katsu, hayai.	Osu, osaeru.	Hineru.
To place, become stiff, embarrassed.	To roll up, lift up.	To conquer, quick.	To press, press upon, print.	To twist, take up, take a pinch of.
捽	捿	掀	掃	授
Sotsu.	Sei.	Kin.	Sō.	Ju.
Tsukamu.	Sumu, sumika.	Sashiageru.	Haku, harau.	Sazukeru.
To grasp.	To dwell, a residence.	To lift up.	To sweep, clear away.	To bestow, give, impart.

掉 × Tō. *Furū.* To shake, brandish.	掌 × Shō. *Tanagokoro, tsukasadoru.* The palm of the hand, to control.	排 × Hai. *Oshihiraku, shirizokeru.* To push open, cause to retire.	掖 × Eki. *Wakibasamu, waki, tasukeru.* To hold under the arm, to assist, quick, the side, side-houses in a palace.	掛 × Kai, Kei. *Kakaru.* To hang up, in suspense. 挂 to concern.
掟 × Jō. *Okite.* A law, decree, ordinance.	掠 × Riaku, Riō. *Toru, kasumeru.* To take, rob.	採 × Sai. *Toru, erabu.* To take, choose, pick.	探 × Tan. *Saguru, sagasu.* To investigate, search for, examine.	掣 × Sei. *Hiku, todomaru.* To pull, stop.
接 × Setsu. *Tsugu, majiwaru, sumiyaka.* To connect, join, associate with, continue, have an interview with, quick.	控 × Kō. *Hikaeru, tsugeru.* To restrain, withdraw, jot down, appeal, accuse.	推 × Sui. *Osu, susumeru.* To push, press, infer, advance.	掩 × En. *Ōu.* To cover, take unawares.	措 × So. *Oku.* To place.
掬 × Kiku. *Sukū.* To scoop up.	捩 × Rei. *Mojiru.* To twist.	揃 × Sen. *Soroeru.* To equalize, match, complete, furnish.	揆 × Ki. *Hakaru.* To plot, plan.	揉 × Jū. *Momu, tameru.* To rub, straighten.
描 × Biō. *Egaku.* To draw, sketch.	提 × Tei. *Hissageru, tazusaeru.* To hold in the hand.	捏 × Detsu, Netsu. *Hineru, koneru.* To twist, knead, mix.	挿 × Sō. *Hasamu, sasu, sashiireru.* To clasp, stick, insert.	揖 × Shū, Yū. *Komanuku, yuzuru.* To fold the hands, yield, bow.
揚 × Yō. *Ageru, arawasu, homeru.* To raise, lift up, hoist, publish, praise.	搾 × Sa. *Shiboru.* To squeeze, milk.	換 × Kwan. *Kaeru.* To change, exchange.	握 × Aku. *Nigiru.* To grasp.	揭 × Kei. *Kakageru.* To lift up, hoist, raise up, publish.

揮 キ.	援 エン.	損 ソン.	搏 ハク, バク
Furū, ugokasu.	Tasukeru, toru, hiku.	Sokonau, ushinau, herasu.	Utsu, toraeru
To shake, wield, scatter.	To assist, rescue, take, cite.	To damage, lose, diminish.	To strike, seize, a
搖 ヨー.	搗 トー.	搜 ソー.	搦 ダク.
Ugokasu, ugoku.	Tsuku.	Sagasu.	Motsu, toru, karameru.
To move.	To pound.	To investigate, search, enquire after.	To hold, take, bi round.
搬 ハン.	摘 テキ.	摧 サイ.	摩 マ.
Nozoku.	Hirou, tsumu.	Kudaku, kujiku.	Suru, migaku, togu.
To take away, transport.	To pick up, pick off.	To break, break in pieces, destroy.	To rub, polish, sharpen.
摺 ショー.	撓 トー.	撒 サン, サツ.	撚 ネン.
Suru, yaburu.	Tawamu.	Chirasu, maku.	Hineru, yoru
To rub, file, print, destroy.	To bend, relax.	To scatter, sow.	To twist, throv (as silk).
撥 ハツ.	撫 ブ.	播 ハ.	撮 サツ, サイ.
Harau, osameru.	Naderu, yasunzuru.	Maku, shiku.	Tsumamu, toru
To scatter, drive away, control.	To stroke, tranquillize.	To sow, spread, publish.	To take a pinch take.
撲 ボク.	撤 テツ.	擁 ヨー.	撿 ケン.
Utsu.	Hagu, toru.	Idaku, kakaeru.	Tsukaneru, ara meru, kangaer
To strike.	To strip off, to take, reject.	To embrace, hold.	To bind, restrain inspect, correct, examine, consider

擅	擇	擊	操	據
Sen.	Taku.	Geki.	Sō.	Kio.
Hoshiimama.	*Erabu.*	*Utsu.*	*Motsu, misao, ayadoru.*	*Yoru, tamotsu.*
As one pleases.	To choose.	To beat, strike.	To hold, chaste, to form the designs on cloth.	To rely on, on account of, to keep.
擒	擘	擔	擡	擢
Kin.	Haku.	Tan.	Tai.	Taku.
Toriko, toraeru.	*Tsunzaku.*	*Ninau.*	*Motageru.*	*Hiku, nukinzuru.*
A captive, to seize, take prisoner.	To break off, tear apart.	To carry on the shoulders, bear, be responsible.	To lift up.	To pull out, excel, select.
擣	擦	擧	擬	擲
Tō.	Satsu.	Kio.	Gi.	Teki.
Utsu, usutsuku.	*Kosuru.*	*Ageru, kozotte, mina.*	*Nazoraeru, hakaru.*	*Nageutsu.*
To strike, pound.	To rub.	To raise, lift up, promote, all.	To imitate, compare, estimate, consult, pass sentence on.	To throw, throw away.
攫	擯	擾	攀	擴
Kwaku.	Hin.	Jō.	Han.	Kwaku.
Toru, nigeru.	*Shirizokeru.*	*Midareru, wazurawashii, nareru.*	*Yojiru.*	*Hirogeru, oshihirogeru.*
To take, grasp.	To cause to retire, reject.	To be confused, disturbed, vexatious, accustomed to.	To climb.	To open, spread out, widen, extend.
攘	擔 携	撕	攣	攪
Jō.	Kei.	Setsu.	Ren.	Kō, kaku.
Harau.	*Tazusaeru, motsu.*	*Toru, kaneru, subemotsu.*	*Tsuru.*	*Midareru, midasu.*
To expel.	To carry in the hand, carry.	To take, do two things at once, act for, direct, administer.	To cramp, be contracted, (as by disease).	Disordered, confused, to derange.
攫	攬			
Kwaku.	Ran.			
Tsukamu.	*Toru, motsu.*			
To grasp, seize.	To take, hold.			

支 夂	支 (The 66th Radical) HAKU. Utsu. To strike.	收 Snū, shu. Osameru, toru, toraeru. To receive, collect, take, reap, pay in (as taxes), seize.	改 KAI. Aratameru, kawaru. To reform, improve, alter, revise, inspect.	攻 Kō. Utsu, semeru. To strike, attack, assault.	孜 SHI. Tsutomeru, hagemu. To exert one's self, labour diligently.
	放 Hō. Hanatsu, hoshii-mama, takuraberu. To let go, banish, as one pleases, to compare.	政 SHI. Matsurigoto, masa-ni, tadashii. Government, political, to govern, just about, correct.	故 Ko. Yue, karugayueni, kotosarani, furui. Because, for this reason, purposely, old, late, formerly.	效 Kō. Narau, manabu, isaoshi. To learn, merit, efficacy.	叙 Jo. Tsuizuru, tsura-naru, noboru. To arrange in order, state, confer rank or title upon.
	教 KIŌ. Oshie, nori, narau, seshimeru. Teaching, doctrine, rule, to learn, cause to do.	敏 BIN. Satoi, toi. Intelligent, quick.	救 KIŪ. Sukū, tasukeru. To save, assist.	敕 CHOKU. Mikotonori. An Imperial command or decree, Imperial.	敗 HAI. Yaburu, sokonau. To break, destroy, defeat.
	赦 SHA. Yurusu, hanatsu. To pardon, let go.	敝 HEI. Tsukareru, yaburu, suteru, tsuzure. To be tired, tear, throw away, rags.	敢 KAN. Aete, isamu. Daring, positively, to be bold, adventurous.	散 SAN. Chiru, chirasu. To scatter.	敦 TON. Atsui, nengoro. Honest, kind, liberal, of consequence.
	敬 KEI, KIŌ. Uyauyashii, uya-mau, tsutsushimu. Reverential, respect-ful, to honour, stand in awe of.	徹 TETSU. Tōru. To pass, pass through.	敲 Kō. Tataku, utsu. To knock, strike, correct.	敵 TEKI. Ada, kataki. An enemy, to oppose.	敷 FU. Shiku. To spread.

數 ✕	整 ✕	斂 ✕	斃 ✕	變 ✕	
Sū.	Sei.	Ren.	Hei.	Hen.	
Kazu, kazoeru, shibashiba, semeru.	Totonoeru, hitoshii.	Osameru, atsumeru.	Taoreru, shinu.	Kawaru, kaeru, wazawai.	
Number, several, to count, often, to press upon.	To put in order, repair, like.	To collect, gather in.	To fall down, die.	To change, alter, transform, calamity, 変 phenomenon.	
文 ✕	斑 ✕				文
(The 67th Radical) Bun, mon. Aya, fumi.	Han. Madara.				
A pattern, ornament, composition, letters, a crest.	Striped, spotted.				
斗 ✕	料 ✕	斛 ✕	斜 ✕	斟 ✕	斗
The 68th Radical) Tō, to. Masu, hoshi.	Riō. Hakaru, motsu.	Koku. —	Sha. Naname.	Shin. Kumu, hakaru.	
A grain or fluid measure equal to about a quarter of an Imperial bushel, the name of a star.	To estimate, fee, price, material.	A koku is a grain measure containing 5.13 bushels 6.53 cubic feet, or 39.70 gallons Imperial Measure.	Slanting.	To draw out, estimate, select.	
斤 ✕	斥 ✕	斧 ✕	斬 ✕	斯 ✕	斤
(The 69th Radical) Kin. Ono.	Seki. Shirizokeru, tōi.	Fu. Ono, yoki.	Zan. Tatsu, kiru.	Shi. Kore, sunawachi, kaku.	
An axe, a catty, (1¼ lbs.)	To drive away, expel, far off.	An axe.	To cut off, cut, behead.	This, that is, namely, thus, so.	
新 ✕	斷 ✕				
Shin. Atarashii, nii, arata.	Dan. Tatsu, kiru, sadameru, kotowaru.				
New, recent, fresh.	To cut off, cut, decide, refuse, decline, give 断 notice.				
方 ✕	於 ✕	施 ✕	旁 ✕	旅 ✕	方
(The 70th Radical) Hō. Kata, keta, tedate.	O. Oite.	Shi, se. Hodokosu.	Hō, nō. Katagata, katawara, amaneku.	Rio. Tabi, moromoro.	
Side, region, direction, person, thing, square, way.	In, on, as to, in regard to.	To give alms, bestow, practise.	One side, while, both, everywhere.	A journey, travelling, a brigade.	

(64)

	旋 ✗ Sen. *Meguru.* To revolve, return.	族 ✗ Zoku. *Yakara, tagui.* Family, relations, persons, sort, kind.	旗 ✗ Ki. *Hata.* A flag.		
无	无 (The 71st Radical) Bu, mu. *Nashi.* Not, without.	既 ✗ Ki. *Sudeni.* Already.			
日	日 ✗ (The 72nd Radical) Jitsu, nichi, nitsu. *Hi.* The sun, day, in the time of.	旦 ✗ Tan. *Ashita, tsuto, akiraka.* The morning, early in the morning, light, clear.	旨 ✗ Shi. *Umai, mune.* Sweet, pleasant to the taste, purport, sense, intention, object, meaning.	早 ✗ Sō. *Ashita, tsuto, hayai.* The morning, early in the morning, early, quick.	旬 ✗ Jun. *Tōka.* A period of ten days, ten.
	旭 ✗ Kioku. *Asahi.* The rising sun.	旱 ✗ Kan. *Hideri.* A drought.	昆 ✗ Kon. *Konokami, onaji.* An elder brother, the same, descendants.	昇 ✗ Shō. *Noboru.* To rise, ascend.	昌 ✗ Shō. *Sakan, akiraka.* Flourishing, bright, clear.
	明 ✗ Mei, miō. *Akiraka, akeru.* Clear, bright, obvious, intelligent, to open, dawn.	昏 ✗ Kon. *Kure, kurai.* The evening, sunset, dark.	易 ✗ I, eki. *Yasui, kaeru.* Easy, to exchange, trade, the art of divining by means of diagrams.	昔 ✗ Seki. *Mukashi, inishie, saki, kinō.* Ancient times, the former times, the past, yesterday.	星 ✗ Sei. *Hoshi.* A star, dot.
	晒 ✗ Sai. *Hosu, sarasu.* To dry in the sun, bleach.	春 ✗ Shun. *Haru.* The Spring.	昧 ✗ Mai. *Kurai, akebono.* Dark, obscure, the dawn, morning twilight.	映 ✗ Ei. *Utsuru.* To reflect as a mirror, shine on.	昨 ✗ Saku. *Kinō, saki.* Yesterday, last.

昭 ✕	是 ✕	時 ✕	晃 ✕	晉
Shō.	Ze, shi.	Ji.	Kwō.	Shin.
Arawareru, akiraka.	*Kore, kokoni, yoi.*	*Toki.*	*Akari, teru.*	*Susumeru.*
To be seen, manifest, revealed, clear.	This, here, good, right.	Time, hour, season.	Light, brightness, to shine.	To advance, increase.
晏	晩 ✕	晝 ✕	晦	晨
An.	Ban.	Chū.	Kwai.	Shin.
Osoi, yawaragu.	*Osoi, kure.*	*Hiru.*	*Kurai, misoka, tsugomori.*	*Tsuto, ashita.*
Late, tranquil.	Late, evening, night.	Noon, day-time.	Dark, the last day of a month.	The morning, early in the morning, dawn.
普 ✕	景 ✕	晴 ✕	晶 ✕	晷
Fu.	Kei.	Sei.	Shō.	Ki.
Amaneku.	*Kage.*	*Hareru.*	*Akiraka, hikari.*	*Hikage.*
All, everywhere.	Shade, sunshine, light, appearance.	To clear up.	Bright, clear, light, crystal.	A sundial or its shadow, day-time.
智 ✕	暄	暇 ✕	暈	暉
Chi.	Ken.	Ka.	Un.	Ki.
Akiraka, satoi, monoshiru.	*Atatakai, nodoka.*	*Hima, itoma.*	*Hi no kasa, tsuki no kasa.*	*Hikari, kagayaku.*
Bright, clear, intelligent, wise.	Warm, genial, mild.	Leisure.	Halo round the sun or moon.	Light, to be bright, flash.
暑 ✕	暖 ✕	暗 ✕	暢 ✕	暮 ✕
Sho.	Dan.	An.	Chō.	Bo.
Atsui.	*Atatakai.*	*Yami, kurai.*	*Nobiru.*	*Kure, kureru.*
Hot, hot weather.	Warm.	Darkness, dark, unintelligent.	To stretch, expand, lengthen.	Evening, sunset, to set.
暱	暴 ✕	暫 ✕	曇 ✕	曆 ✕
Jitsu.	Bō, boku.	Zan.	Don.	Reki.
Chikazuku, mutsumajii.	*Arai, niwaka, sarasu.*	*Shibaraku.*	*Kumoru.*	*Koyomi.*
To draw near, intimate.	Violent, riotous, sudden, to expose to the sun.	A short time, some time.	To be cloudy.	An almanach.

日	曉 Kiō. Akatsuki, ashita, satosu. The dawn, daybreak, morning, to perceive, know.	曙 Sho. Akebono. Morning twilight.	曜 Yō. Hikari. Light, day.	曠 Kwō. Munashii, hiroi. Empty, void, futile, wide, vast.	曩 Dō, Nō, Jō. Mukashi, sakini. Ancient times, previously.
	曰 (The 73th Radical) Etsu. Iu, iwaku. To speak, say, call.	曲 Kioku. Magaru, yugamu. To bend, crooked.	曳 Ei. Hiku, nobiru. To pull, drag, extend.	更 Kō. Kawaru, aratamaru, sarani. To change, reform, again, quite, a watch in the night.	沓 Tō. Kasanaru. To be piled up, increase in bulk or numbers.
	曷 Katsu. Yameru, nanzo, izukunzo. To stop, how? why?	書 Sho. Kaku, shirusu, fumi. To write, a book, letter, document.	曹 Sō. Tomogara, moromoro. A collective noun used to form the plural, persons, a company.	曾 Sō. Katsute. Before, previously.	替 Tai. Kawaru, sutaru. To change, substitute, be discarded, out of use.
	最 Sai. Mottomo. Very, best, right.	會 Kwai, E. Atsumeru, au. A meeting, company, to assemble, meet.			
月	月 (The 74th Radical) Getsu, Gwatsu. Tsuki. The moon, month.	有 U, Yū. Aru, tamotsu. To be, have, keep, possess.	朋 Hō. Tomo. A friend, companion.	服 Fuku. Kimono, shitagau. Clothing, the numeral for doses of medicine or whiffs of tobacco, to obey.	朔 Saku. Tsuitachi, kita. The first day of a month, the North.
	朕 Chin. Ware. The Imperial "We."	朗 Rō. Hogaraka. Bright, clear, spacious.	望 Bō, Mō. Nozomi. To desire, hope, expect, full moon.	朝 Chō. Asa, tsuto, ashita. The morning, early, dawn, the Emperor, Court, Government, one's own country.	期 Ki. Ataru, toki, chigiru. A period of time, fixed time, to fix.

朦 ヤ	朧 ヤ				
Mō, Bō.	Rō.				
Oboro.	*Oboro.*				
Dim, cloudy, obscure.	Dim, cloudy, obscure.				
木 ヤ	未 ヤ	末 ヤ	本 ヤ	札 ヤ	木
(The 75th Radical) Boku, moku. Ki.	Mi, bi.	Matsu, batsu.	Hon.	Satsu.	
A tree, wood.	*Imada, arazu, hitsuji.*	*Sue.*	*Moto, hajime.*	*Fuda, wakajini.*	
	Not yet, not, the goat (the 8th of the twelve horary characters).	The end, the top branch, a descendant, future.	The origin, beginning, principal, real, single, this, a book, a numeral for long round articles.	A ticket, card, note, paper money, early death.	
朱 ヤ	朴 ヤ	朶	机 ヤ	朽 ヤ	
Shu.	Boku.	Da.	Ki.	Kiū.	
Akai.	*Ki no kawa.*	*Eda.*	*Tsukue, oshimazuki.*	*Kuchiru.*	
Red, vermilion, red ink.	The bark of a tree, plain, simple.	A branch, cluster.	A table, desk, stand for resting against.	To decay.	
杆	杉 ヤ	李 ヤ	杣 ヤ	杏	
Kan.	San.	Ri.	Sen.	Kiō.	
Teko.	*Sugi.*	*Sumomo.*	*Soma.*	*Anzu.*	
A lever.	The cedar, Cryptomeria.	A plum.	A woodman, wood-cutter.	An apricot.	
材 ヤ	村 ヤ	杓 ヤ	杖 ヤ	杙	
Sai, zai.	Son.	Shaku.	Jō.	Yoku.	
Tsukurigi.	*Mura.*	*Hitsu.*	*Tsue.*	*Kui.*	
Material, stuff, timber, lumber, qualities.	A village.	A dipper, ladle, to draw (as water).	A cane, stick.	A stake, pile.	
束 ヤ	枡	杭 ヤ	柿 ヤ	盃 ヤ	
Soku.	Shō.	Kō.	Shi.	Hai.	
Tsukaneru.	*Masu.*	*Kui.*	*Kaki.*	*Sakazuki.*	
To tie, bind.	A wooden box for measuring liquids, etc.	A stake, pile.	A persimmon. 柿	A wine-cup, glass. 盃	

東 ✗	杵	杼	松 ✗	板 ✗
Tō.	Sho.	Jo.	Shō.	Han.
Higashi, azuma.	Kine.	Tochi, hi.	Matsu.	Ita.
The East, the Eastern Provinces.	A pestle, mallet.	The horse-chestnut, a shuttle.	The pine.	A board, printing block.
枉	析	枕 ✗	林 ✗	枚 ✗
Ō.	Seki.	Chin.	Rin.	Bai, mai.
Mageru, magete.	Wakatsu.	Makura.	Hayashi.	Eda, kazu.
To bend, distort, condescendingly.	To divide, separate, analyse.	A pillow.	A forest.	A stem, one (used of flat objects), to number.
果 ✗	枝 ✗	牀	柝	枯 ✗
Kwa.	Shi.	Shō.	Taku.	Ko.
Hatasu, ki no mi.	Eda.	Yuka, toko.	Hiōshigi.	Kareru.
To end, accomplish, fruit.	A branch.	The floor, boards, a bed, couch.	Clappers.	To be dried, withered, dead.
査 ✗	架 ✗	枷	柁	柄 ✗
Sa.	Ka, ga.	Ka.	Ta, da.	Hei.
Uki-ki, ikada.	Kakeru, tana.	Kubigase.	Kaji.	Tsuka, e.
A raft, to enquire into (officially).	To put up, erect, a shelf.	The cangue.	A rudder.	A handle.
某 †	柊 ✗	柏 ✗	柔 ✗	柑
Bō.	Tō.	Haku.	Jū, niū.	Kan.
Soregashi.	Hiragi.	Kashiwa.	Yawaraka.	Tachibana no tagui
A certain person, I.	Holly.	An oak.	Soft, gentle, tender.	An orange.

栓	栅	栖	栗	校
Sen.	Saku.	Sei.	Ritsu.	Kō.
Koroppo, kikugi.	Shigarami.	Sumu, sumika.	Kuri.	Kangaeru, shirabe-ru, mono manabi-dokoro.
A stopper, cork, wooden peg.	Hurdles, piles, a palisade.	To reside, roost, a dwelling.	A chestnut.	To consider, compare, examine, revise, a school.
株	核	根	格	栽
Chu.	Kaku, kai.	Kon.	Kaku.	Sai.
Kabu, kuize.	Sane.	Ne, moto.	Itaru, tadashii.	Ueru.
The stump of a tree, the numeral for trees, &c., a share, stocks.	The seeds of fruit, plates of armour, a gland.	The root, origin.	Rank, station, pattern, rule, the object in grammar, to reach, correct, right.	To plant.
桁	桂	桔	桃	案
Kō.	Kei.	Ketsu.	Tō.	An.
Keta.	Katsura.	Hanetsurube.	Momo.	Tsukue, kangaeru.
Cross beams.	The olea fragrans.	A well-bucket.	A peach.	Table, bar, bench before a judge, law case, opinion, expectation.
桎	桐	桑	梅	椰
Shitsu.	Tō.	Sō.	Bai.	Ya.
Ashigase.	Kiri.	Kuwa.	Ume.	Yashi.
Stocks, fetters.	A tree (the Paullownia Imperialis).	The mulberry.	A plum.	A cocoanut.
桶	梁	梃	條	梟
Tō.	Riō.	Chō.	Jō.	Kiō.
Oke.	Hari, yana.	Tsue.	Koeda.	Fukurō.
A bucket.	Rafters, the long beams of a bridge, a bridge, weir, basket for catching fish.	A cane, stick, the numeral for guns, vehicles, candles, &c.	A twig, an article, item.	An owl.
梢	梨	梯	械	梳
Shō.	Ri.	Tei.	Kai.	Sho.
Kozue.	Nashi.	Hashigo.	Ashigase.	Kushikezuru.
A twig.	A pear.	A ladder.	Fetters, an instrument, machine.	To comb.

梵 BON. *Kiyoi.* Brahma, Sanscrit, sacred.	棄 KI. *Suteru, sutaru.* To throw away, reject, abandoned, obsolete.	棲 SEI. *Sumu, sumika.* To reside, roost, a dwelling, perch.	棒 BŌ. *Tsuie.* A pole, bar.
棟 TŌ. *Mune, munagi.* The ridge of a roof.	棧 SAN. *Kakehashi.* A suspension-bridge, pier.	棺 KWAN. *Hitsugi.* A coffin.	森 SHIN. *Mori, saka[?]* A wood, flourish[?]
椀 WAN. — A bowl (of wood).	椅 I. — 子 A chair.	植 SHOKU. *Ueru.* To plant, set, colonize, inoculate.	椎 SUI. *Shii.* The oak (quer[cus] cuspidata).
椽 EN. *Taruki.* The timbers of a roof, rafters.	椿 CHIN. *Tsubaki.* A camellia.	楊 YŌ. *Yanagi.* A willow.	楓 FŪ. *Momiji, kae[?]* The maple.
楢 YŪ. *Nara.* The evergreen oak.	楫 SHŪ. *Kaji.* A rudder, oar, paddle.	業 GIŌ, GŌ. *Shiwaza, nariwai.* Calling, occupation, business.	楮 CHO. *Kōzu.* The paper mult[?]
極 KIOKU, GOKU. *Kiwameru.* Very, extremely, to determine, fix, exhaust, investigate thoroughly.	楷 KAI. *Nori.* A model, the square character.	榴 RIŪ. *Jakuro.* The pomegranate.	榛 SHIN. *Hashibami* The hazel, Cory[lus] heterophylla

榮 ✕ **Ei.** *Sakae, hiideru.* Splendour, to be luxuriant, excellent, to surpass.	樣 ✕ **Yō.** *Sama.* Manner, form, appearance, Mr.	構 ✕ **Kō.** *Kamae, kamaeru.* The external appearance, an enclosure, attitude, to devise, construct.	槙 **Ten, shin.** *Maki.* A kind of fir (Podocarpus chinensis).	槌 **Tai, tsui.** *Tsuchi, utsu.* A hammer, mallet, to strike.
槩 ✕ **Gai.** *Ōmune.* Generally, for the most part.	樂 ✕ **Gaku, raku.** *Tanoshimi.* Happiness, delight, pleasure, comfort, music.	標 ✕ **Hiō.** *Shirushi, arawasu.* A mark, sign, to display.	樅 **Shō.** *Momi.* A kind of fir.	樋 ✕ **Tō.** *Toi, hi.* A water pipe, spout, faucet.
樓 ✕ **Rō.** *Takadono.* A house of two or more storeys, the second storey, a brothel.	樞 **Sū.** *Toboso, kururu.* A hinge, pivot, important, essential.	槻 **Ki.** *Keyaki, tsuki.* A tree, a species of Zelkowa.	樟 ✕ **Shō.** *Kusu.* The camphor tree.	樫 **Ken.** *Kashi.* The oak.
樵 **Shō.** *Kikori.* A wood-cutter.	樸 ✕ **Boku.** *Sunao, kiji.* Plain, simple, honest, unvarnished.	樹 ✕ **Ju.** *Ki, ueru, tateru.* A tree, to plant, erect.	樺 **Kwa.** *Kaba.* The birch, reddish brown.	橲 ✕ **Son.** *Taru.* A barrel.
橇 **Sei.** *Sori.* A sleigh.	橋 ✕ **Kiō.** *Hashi.* A bridge.	橘 **Kitsu.** *Tachibana.* A general term for oranges.	橙 **Tō.** *Daidai.* A kind of bitter orange.	機 ✕ **Ki.** *Hata, hazumi, ayatsuri.* A loom, spring, impulse, chance, machinery, important.
橡 **Shō.** *Tochi.* The horse-chestnut.	橫 ✕ **Kwō, Ō.** *Yoko, hoshiimama, yokotau.* Across, self-willed, to place across.	檄 **Geki.** *Meshibumi, satoshibumi* A summons, circular, manifesto.	檉 **Tei.** *Kawayanagi.* The river-willow.	檢 **Ken.** *Shirusu, fumi, kangaeru.* An envelope, case, model, to examine.

(72)

檎	簷	檀	檜	檣
Kin.	En.	Dan.	Kwai.	Shō.
Ringo.	Noki.	Mayumi.	Hinoki.	Hobashira.
An apple.	The eaves of a house.	The sandal wood tree much prized by the priests, hence a Buddhist temple.	A species of pine (Thuya obtusa).	A mast.
檻	櫂	櫓	櫛	櫻
Kan.	Tō.	Ro.	Shitsu.	Ō.
Ori.	Kai.	Yagura.	Kushi.	Sakura.
A cage, prison.	An oar, skull.	A watch-tower, wooden turret, upper deck of a ship.	A comb.	The cherry.
欄	權			
Ran.	Ken, gon.			
Obashima.	Kari ni, hakaru.			
A balustrade, railing, enclosure, columns (of a newspaper).	Power, authority, influence, temporary, assistant, vice, to plan.			
欠 (The 76th Radical)	次	欣	欲	欺
Ken, ketsu.	Ji.	Kin.	Yoku.	Ki.
Akubi, kaku.	Tsugi, tsugu.	Yorokobu.	Hossuru, yokubaru.	Azamuku.
To yawn, deficient, to owe money.	Next, assistant, vice, to succeed.	To rejoice.	To wish, desire, covet, lust.	To deceive, cheat
欽	款	歉	歌	歐
Kin.	Kwan.	Ken.	Ka.	Ō.
Tsutsushimu.	Makoto, tataku.	Akitarazu, uramu.	Uta, utau.	Haku.
To be respectful, Imperial.	True, a section, sincere, an article, to strike.	Unsatisfied, insufficient, to covet, envy.	A song, poem, to sing.	To vomit.
歟	歡			
Yo.	Kwan.			
Ka.	Yorokobu.			
An interrogative particle.	To rejoice.			

(73)

止 ✕ (The 77th Radical) SHI. *Yamu, todomaru.* To stop, cease, remain.	正 ✕ SEI, SHŌ. *Tadashii, masa ni, tsukasa.* Correct, straight, just, proper, legal, a ruler, chief.	此 ✕ SHI. *Kore, koko, koko ni.* This, here.	步 ✕ HO, BU. *Ayumu, funa-tsuki.* To walk, a step, a land measure of six feet, a *tsubo*, interest, a jetty.	武 ✕ BU, MU. *Takei, tsuyoi.* Military, fierce, strong.	止
岐 KI. *Futamata, chimata.* Cross roads, forks in a road.	歪 AI. *Yokoshima, yugamu.* Evil, to be inclined from the right direction, crooked.	歲 ✕ SAI. *Toshi.* A year.	歷 ✕ REKI. *Heru.* To pass, successive, eminent, prominent.	歸 ✕ KI. *Kaeru.* To return, revert, end.	
歹 (The 78tlr Radical) KATSU. *Sarebone.* Dry bones.	死 ✕ SHI. *Shinu.* Death, to die, the dead.	殄 TEN. *Horobu, tatsu.* To exterminate, finish, destroy.	殁 ✕ BOTSU, MOTSU. *Shinu.* To die, the dead.	殀 YŌ. *Wakajini.* Early death.	歹
殂 So. *Shinu, owaru.* To die (used of a prince), end.	殆 ✕ TAI. *Hotondo.* In great danger, almost, greatly.	殉 JUN. *Shitagau, okuru.* To follow, (even unto death), accompany in death (used of human sacrifices), die for another.	殊 ✕ SHU. *Koto ni, korosu, wakatsu.* Especially, to kill, distinguish.	殖 ✕ SHOKU. *Fuyasu.* To increase, enlarge, get rich.	
殘 ✕ ZAN. *Nokoru, sokonau.* To be left over, injure, destroy.	殤 SHŌ. *Wakajini.* An early death.	斃 HEI. *Taoreru.* To fall, die.	殯 HIN. *Karimogari.* Temporary burial.		
殳 (The 79th Radical) SHU. *Hoko.* A spear.	段 ✕ DAN, TAN. ― A step, grade, plat-form section, subject, 300 *tsubos* of land.	殷 IN. *Sakan, akai.* Flourishing, red.	殺 ✕ SATSU, SETSU. *Korosu, kiru, sogu.* To kill, cut, slice off.	殻 KAKU. *Kara.* The shell, skin.	殳

	殿 × Den. *Tono, dono, shingari.* An Imperial Palace, palace, temple, lord, Mr., the rearguard of an army.	毀 × Ki. *Kobotsu, yaburu, soshiru.* To break, destroy, slander.	殷 × Kō. *Tataku.* To strike, knock.	毅 × Ki. *Tsuyoi, takei.* Strong, firm, stern.	毆 × Ō. *Utsu, tataku.* To strike, knock, assault.
毋	毋 (The 80th Radical) Bu, mu, bō. *Nashi, nakare.* A prohibitive negative adverb, not, do not.	母 × Bo, bō. *Haha.* A mother.	每 × Mai. *Goto ni, tsune ni.* Every, each, always.	毒 × Doku. — Poison.	
比	比 × (The 81st Radical) Hi. *Tagui, takuraberu, naraberu.* Sort, kind, to compare, arrange in a row, bring into harmony.	毗 × Hi. *Tasukeru, atsui.* To assist, kind, liberal. 毘			
毛	毛 × (The 82nd Radical) Mō. *Ke.* Hair, fur, feathers.	毬 × Kiū. *Mari.* A ball, balloon.	毫 × Gō. *Ke, hosoi, sukoshi.* A hair's breadth, thin, a very little.	麾 × Ki. *Sashimaneku, kobata.* To beckon, a small flag for signalling.	氈 × Sen. *Kemushiro.* A woollen rug.
氏	氏 × (The 83rd Radical) Shi. *Uji.* Surname, Mr.	民 × Min. *Tami.* The people.			
气	气 × (The 84th Radical) Ki, kitsu. *Iki.* Breath, vapour.	氣 × Ki, ke. *Iki.* Vapour, breath, spirit, mood.			

水 ✕	氷 ✕	永 ✕	汀 ✕	汁 ✕
(The 85th Radical) SUI. Mizu. Water.	HIŌ. Kōri. Ice.	EI. Nagai, hisashii. Long, a long time, everlasting.	TEI. Migiwa, nagisa, susaki. The beach, a sandy spit, isthmus.	SHŪ. Shiru. Juice, gravy
求 ✕	汎 ✕	汐 ✕	汗 ✕	汝 ✕
KIŪ. Motomeru. To seek, ask for, get.	HAN. Ukabu, tadayou, hiroi. To float, drift about, wide.	SEKI. Shio. The evening tide, tide.	KAN. Ase. Sweat.	JO. Nanji, imashi. You.
汞	江 ✕	池 ✕	汚 ✕	汰 ✕
KŌ. Mizukane. Mercury, quicksilver.	KŌ. E. A river, arm of the sea.	CHI. Ike. A pond.	O. Kegareru. To be dirty, polluted.	TA, TAI. Soroeru, furū. To arrange properly sift by shaking, cleanse correct.
汲 ✕	決 ✕	沃 ✕	沈 ✕	沐 ✕
KIŪ. Kumu. To draw water, busy.	KETSU. Wakeru, sadameru. To settle, determine, decide.	YOKU. Uruou, sakan, sosogu. To be moist, rich, to wash.	CHIN. Shizumu, hitasu. To sink, be immersed.	MOKU. Kami-arau. To wash the hair, bathe.
没 ✕	沓	沙 ✕	沫	沮
BOTSU, MOTSU. Oboreru, owaru. To sink, drown, end, die.	TŌ. Midari, musaboru. Irregular, disorderly, avaritious.	SA, SHA. Suna, isago. Sand.	MATSU. Awa. A bubble.	SHO, SO. Habamu, todomeru. To oppose, prevent, stop.
河 ✕	沸 ✕	油 ✕	治 ✕	沼 ✕
KA. Kawa. A river.	FUTSU. Waku. To boil up.	YU. Abura. Oil.	CHI, JI. Osameru, kangaeru. To govern, tranquilize, consider, try (as a legal cause).	SHŌ. Numa. A marsh.

(76)

沾 Ko. Kau, uru. To buy, sell.	沿 En. Sou. To go by the side of, follow a stream, successive.	泄 Ei. Moru. To leak.	泅 Shū. Oyogu. To swim, float.	泉 Sen. Izumi. A spring.
泊 Haku. Todomaru, tomaru, tadayou. To stop, lodge, drift.	法 Hō. Nori, nottoru. A law, rule, doctrine, to follow the example of.	泛 Han. Ukabu. To float.	泡 Hō. Awa. A bubble.	波 Ha. Nami. A wave.
泣 Kiū. Naku. To cry, weep.	泥 Dei. Doro, nazumu. Mud, to adhere to, be addicted to.	注 Chū. Sosogu. To water, wash, give heed to.	泰 Tai. Yutaka, ōinaru, yasui. Fertile, large, great, calm, pacific.	泳 Ei. Oyogu, mizu-kuguru. To swim, dive.
泯 Min. Horobu. To be destroyed, ruined.	洋 Yō. Sakan, ōumi. Flourishing, the Ocean.	洒 Sai. Sosogu, arau. To sprinkle water on, wash.	洗 Sen. Arau. To wash.	洛 Raku. Miyako. The Capital.
洞 Dō. Hora, fukai, hogaraka. A cave, deep, clear.	洽 Gō. Amaneku. Universally, all.	洲 Shū. Su. A delta, islet, continent.	津 Shin. Tsu, watari. A harbour, ford.	洪 Kō. Ōi naru, ō-mizu. Great, a flood.
洵 Jun. Makoto, hitoshii. Truth, alike, equal.	洩 Ei. Moru. To leak.	活 Kwatsu. Ikiru. To be alive, active, moveable.	派 Ha. Eda-nagare. A branch, stream, sect, party.	浚 Shun. Sarau. To dredge, clean out.

浦 † Ho. *Ura.* The sea-coast.	浩 Kō. *Hiroi, ōinaru.* Wide, large, great.	浪 × Rō. *Nami, midarini.* A wave, disorderly, vagrant, unattached.	浮 × Fu. *Ukabu, uku, uki.* To float, light, fickle, a buoy.	浴 † Yoku. *Abiru.* To bathe, wash the body.	
浸 † Shin. *Hitasu, shizumeru.* To soak, sink.	消 † Shō. *Kieru, kesu.* To disappear, extinguish, erase.	涉 Shō. *Wataru.* To cross over, ford, spend (as time), acquainted with.	涌 † Yō. *Waku.* To boil. 湧	涎 Zen, en. *Yodare.* Saliva.	
涕 Tei. *Namida.* Tears.	流 × Riū, ru. *Nagareru, tagui.* To flow, a sort, kind, to circulate, spread, transport criminals.	涜 × Kwan. *Arau.* To wash.	海 × Kai. *Umi.* The sea.	涅 Detsu, netsu, ne. *Kuri ni suru.* To make muddy, defile.	
染 † Sen. *Someru.* To dye.	涯 † Gai. *Migiwa, hotori, kagiri, kishi.* Margin, boundary, bank.	液 † Eki. *Shiru.* Juice.	涵 † Kan. *Hitasu.* To soak.	涸 Ko. *Kareru.* To dry up (as a channel) to become skilful (as in penmanship).	
淀 Ten. *Yodo, yodomi.* An eddy, stagnation, hesitation in speaking.	淋 Rin. *Shitataru.* To drip.	淑 † Shuku. *Yawarageru, yoi.* To soften, harmonize, good, gentle, virtuous.	淚 × Rui. *Namida.* Tears.	淡 × Tan. *Awai, usui.* Of delicate flavour, tasteless, flat, fresh, thin.	
淨 † Jō. *Kiyoi, isagiyoi.* Pure, clear.	渝 Rin. *Sazanami, shizumu.* A ripple, to sink.	淫 † In. *Nagaame, midara, fukeru.* Long-continued rain, arbitrary, wanton, lewd, addicted to.	深 † Shin. *Fukai.* Deep.	淳 † Jun. *Sunao, tadashii.* Honest, virtuous.	

淵	混 †	清 †	淺 †	添
EN.	KON.	SEI.	SEN.	TEN.
Fuchi.	Majiru.	Kiyoi.	Asai.	Sou.
A deep pool, eddy, whirlpool, abyss.	To mix.	Pure, clear.	Shallow.	To add, supplement, annex, enclose.
渚 †	減 ×	渠	渡 †	渥
SHO.	GEN.	KIO.	To.	AKU.
Nagisa.	Heru.	Hiroi, nanzo.	Wataru, watari.	Atsui, uruou.
A beach, shore.	To decrease, subtract. 減	Wide, how, why, an aqueduct, dock.	To cross over, send, deliver, pay, diametre, a ferry.	Thick, great, liberal.
渦	渫	測 †	港 ×	渇
KWA.	SETSU.	SOKU.	KŌ.	KATSU.
Uzumaku, uzu.	Sarau.	Hakaru.	Minato.	Kawaku.
To whirl round, a whirlpool, eddy.	To clear out, dredge.	To measure, survey.	A harbour.	Thirst, to be dry.
游 †	渺	渾	湊 †	温
YŪ.	BIŌ.	KON.	SŌ.	ON.
Oyogu.	Haruka, kasuka.	Subete, madoka.	Minato, atsumaru.	Atataka, atsui.
To swim.	Distant, indistinct.	All, quite, round.	A harbour, to assemble.	Warm, hot.
湖 †	湛	湮	湯 ×	源 ×
KO.	TAN.	IN.	TŌ.	GEN.
Mizuumi.	Tataeru, hitasu.	Uzumu, ochiru.	Yu.	Minamoto.
A lake.	To fill, soak.	To bury, die, cease.	Hot water.	The source.
準 ×	湎 †	溝 †	溟	溢 †
JUN.	RIŌ.	KŌ.	MEI.	ITSU.
Hakaru, nazorau, nori.	Tamaru.	Mizo.	Umi, kurai.	Afureru.
To measure, make like, compare, adjust, rules.	To collect, accumulate.	A ditch, drain.	The sea, dark, deep.	To overflow.

(79)

溶	溺 ✕	滅 ✕	汽 ✕
Yō.	Deki.	Metsu.	Ki.
kiagaru, nagareru, tokasu.	Oboreru.	Horobu, kieru, taeru.	—
To boil up, melt, dissolve.	To drown, sink, floating on.	To be destroyed, ruined, extinct.	Steam.
滑 ✕	滯 ✕	漕 ✕	滴 ✕
Watsu, Kotsu.	Tai.	Sō.	Teki.
Nameraka.	Todokōru, todomaru.	Kogu, hakobu.	Shitataru.
slippery, smooth, flattering.	To be obstructed, stop, stay.	To row, scull, transport.	To drip.
滿 ✕	漁 ✕	漂 ✕	漉
Man.	Gio.	Hiō.	Roku.
Michiru.	Sunadoru.	Tadayou.	Kosu.
be full, satisfied, complete.	To fish.	To drift.	[To filter.
漑	演 ✕	漠 ✕	漢 ✕
Gai, ki.	En.	Baku.	Kan.
Sosogu.	Noberu, nagareru.	Hiroi.	Amanogawa, onoko.
sprinkle, wash.	To speak, lecture, flow.	Wide, obscure.	The milky way, a man, the name of an ancient Chinese Kingdom, China.
漫 ✕	漬 ✕	漆 ✕	漲
Man.	Shi.	Shitsu.	Chō.
izu, midarini, habikoru.	Hitasu, tsukeru.	Urushi.	Minagiru.
flood, arbitrarily, without leave, to spread.	To soak, pickle.	Lacquer.	To surge, swell up.
澆	潛 ✕	潤	潦
Gio.	Sen.	Jun.	Rō, riō.
Sosogu.	Hisomu, kuguru.	Uruou.	Tamarimizu, niwatazumi.
sprinkle, irrigate, wash, perfidious.	To hide, dive.	To be moist, rich.	A puddle.

潮 ✕	潰 ✕	澄 ✕	潔 ✕	澁 ✕
Chō.	Kwai.	Chō.	Ketsu.	Shū.
Ushio.	Tsuieru, tsubureru.	Sumu.	Isagiyoi.	Shibu, shiburu.
The water of the ocean, tide, opportunity.	To run out (as water), break.	To be clear.	Pure, clean, holy.	Sap, to be astringent, obstructed.

澤 ✕	澱	激 ✕	濁 ✕	濃 ✕
Taku.	Den.	Geki.	Daku.	Nō.
Sawa, uruou.	Doro, odomi, yodo.	Minagiru, tsukiataru.	Nigoru.	Koi, komayaka.
A valley, marsh, to be moist, rich.	Mud, mire, dregs, still water.	To be excited, fierce, surge up, rush against.	To be muddy, a sonant.	Thick, deep, strong, minute.

濕 +	濘	濟 +	濡 ✕	濫
Shitsu, Shū.	Nei.	Sai.	Ju.	Ran.
Uruou, nureru.	Doro.	Wataru, sukū, sumasu.	Nureru, hitasu.	Hitasu, midari.
To be moist, wet.	Mud.	To cross over, save, settle.	To be wet, soak.	To soak, irregularly.

濤 +	濯 +	濱 ✕	濆 ✕	瀉
Tō.	Taku.	Hin.	Toku.	Sha.
Ūnami.	Arau, susugu.	Hama, hotori, migiwa.	Sosogu, kegasu, nigoru.	Sosogu, kata.
Great waves, billows.	To wash, sprinkle.	The sea-coast, beach, near the sea.	To sprinkle, defile, muddy.	To sprinkle, a beach.

瀑 ✕	瀧 ✕	瀨 ✕	瀰	瀾
Baku.	Rō.	Rai.	Bi.	Ran.
Taki.	Taki.	Se.	Michiru, nagareru.	Ūnami, nagareru.
A waterfall.	A waterfall.	A stream, channel, shoal, rapids.	To be full, flow, abundance.	Big waves, to flow.

灌	灑 ✕	灘 ✕	灣 ✕	
Kwan.	Sai.	Dan, Nan.	Wan.	
Sosogu, arau.	Sosogu.	Nada, se.	Mizu no kuma.	
To sprinkle, wash.	To sprinkle, pour into, wash.	A sea, a portion of the sea with strong waves.	A bay.	

火 ✕	灰 ✕	炎 ✕	災 ✕	炙 ✕	火
(The 86th Radical) KWA. HI. Fire.	KWAI. Hai. Ashes.	KIŌ. Yaito, yaku. The moxa, to cauterize.	SAI. Wazawai. Calamity.	SHA, SEKI. Aburu. To fire, roast, warm, cauterize.	
炊 ✕	炎 ✕	畑 ✕	炬 ✕	炭 ✕	
SUI. Kashigu. To cook rice.	EN. Honō, atsu. A flame, hot.	— Hata, hatake. A field, vegetable garden.	KIO. Taimatsu, akai. A torch, red.	TAN. Sumi. Charcoal.	
烈 ✕	烏 ✕	烙 ✕	烝 ✕	烟 ✕	
RETSU. Hageshii, atsui. Violent, hot, ardent.	A, U. Karasu, kuroi, aa. A crow, black, an exclamation, interrogative particle.	RAKU. Aburu. To fire, roast, warm, brand.	JŌ. Moromoro, susumeru, musu. All, a multitude, to advance, steam.	EN. Kemuri. Smoke.	
烽 ✕	焉 ✕	焙 ✕	焦 ✕	焚 ✕	
HŌ. Kagaribi, noroshi. A beacon, signal rocket or fire.	EN. Izukunzo, nanzo, kokoni. How ? why ? here, also, used as an affirmative final particle.	HAI, HŌ. Aburu, hōjiru. To fire, roast, warm.	SHŌ. Kogasu. To char, scorch.	FUN. Yaku, taku. To burn.	
無 ✕	焰 ✕	然 ✕	輝 ✕	煉 ✕	
BU, MU. Nai. Not.	EN. Honō-o. A flame.	ZEN, NEN. Moyasu, shikaru. To burn, be so, an adverbial particle implying yes, but, however.	KI. Kagayaku. To glitter, shine.	REN. Neru, kitaeru. To temper, forge.	
煙 ✕	煮 ✕	煎 ✕	熙 ✕	煖 ✕	
EN. Kemuri. Smoke.	SHO. Niru. To boil.	SEN. Iru. To fire, roast.	KI. Hiromaru, hiroi, yawaragu. To widen, wide, to soften, harmonize.	DAN. Atatameru, atataka. To warm, warm.	

煤 BAI. Susu. Soot.	**照** SHŌ. Terasu, akiraka. To illuminate, clear, bright, to compare, agree with (as a precedent).	**煩** HAN. Wazurawasu. To vex, trouble, be ill.	**煠** SHŌ. Yuderu, yaku, yubiku. To boil, burn, scald.	**熄** SHOKU. Kieru. To disappear, go out.
煽 SEN. Hi wo okosu, aogu. To kindle a fire, fan, stir up, incite to sedition.	**熊** YŪ. Kuma. A bear.	**熟** JUKU. Umu, tsuratsura. To ripen, mature, thoroughly, carefully.	**熬** GŌ. Iru. To roast, fire.	**熱** NETSU. Atsui. Hot, heat, fever.
熾 SHI. Moyeru, sakan. To burn, flourishing, great.	**燃** ZEN, NEN. Moyeru. To burn.	**燈** TŌ. Tomoshibi. A light, lamp, lantern.	**燐** RIN. Kitsunebi. Ignis fatuus, phosphorus.	**燒** SHŌ. Yaku. To burn.
燧 SUI. Uchibi, noroshi. Fire produced by a flint and steel, a beacon.	**燔** HAN. Yaku, aburu. To burn, fire, warm.	**燕** EN. Tsubame. A swallow.	**營** EI. Ie, itonamu. A camp, to make, perform, build, business, occupation.	**燥** SŌ. Kawaku. To dry.
燭 SHOKU, SOKU. Terasu, tomoshibi. To give light, a light, candle.	**燹** SEN. Moeru, wazawai. To burn, a calamity, conflagration.	**燻** KUN. Kusuberu. To smoke, fumigate.	**燼** JIN. Moegui. A charred piece of wood, firebrand, faggot.	**爆** BAKU. Atsui, yaku. Hot, to burn, explode.
爛 RAN. Tadareru, akiraka. To be inflamed, clear, bright.	**爐** RO. Irori. A hearth, fireplace.			

爪	爭	爰	爲	爵
(The 87th Radical) Sō. *Tsume.* Nails, hoofs, claws, talons.	Sō. *Arasou, kisou.* To contend, compete, dispute about, wrangle, litigate.	En. *Koko ni.* Here, therefore, thereupon.	I. *Tame, tsukuru, nasu.* For the sake of, for, by, to, to make, do, used as a causative verb.	Shaku. *Kurai.* Rank, title, order of nobility.
父	爺			
(The 88th Radical) Fu, Ho. *Chichi.* A father.	Ya. *Chichi, toshiyori.* A father, old man.			
爻	爽	爾		
(The 89th Radical) Kō. *Majiwaru.* To mix.	Sō. *Akiraka, sawaaka, isagiyoi.* Clear, pure, fluent, cheerful.	Ji. *Nanji, shikari, chikai.* You, just so, near.		
爿	牆			
(The 90th Radical) Han, Shō. *Katami.* One side, one of two.	Shō. *Kakine.* A wall, fence.			
片	版	牒		
(The 91st Radical) Hen, Han. *Katagata.* One side.	Han. *Fuda, ita.* Records, a schedule, registers, a printing or engraving block.	Chō. *Fuda.* A tablet, record, despatch.		
牙	撑			
(The 92nd Radical) Ga, Ge. *Kiba.* A tooth.	Tō. *Sasaeru.* To prop up, ward off, support.			

牛 ✕	牝 ✕	牡 ✕	牢 ✕	牧 ✕
(The 93rd Radical) GIŪ. *Ushi*. An ox, cow, bull, cattle.	HIN. *Mesu*. The female of birds and animals.	BO. *Osu*. The male of birds and animals.	RŌ. *Katai, hitoya, ori*. Hard, strong, a jail, cage.	BOKU, MOKU. *Maki, yashinau*. Pasture land, to rear, breed, foster.
物 ✕	牲 ✕	特 ✕	牽 ✕	犀
BUTSU, MOTSU. *Mono*. A thing, matter, article.	SEI. *Ikenie*. Animal sacrifices.	TOKU. *Koto ni, tada, hitori*. Especially, only, alone.	KEN. *Hiku, tsuranaru*. To pull, conduct, be related to.	SAI. *Katai*. The rhinoceros, hard.
犂	犒	犢		
RI. *Karasuki, madara-ushi*. A plough, a spotted ox.	KŌ. *Negirau*. To entertain.	TOKU. *Koushi*. A calf.		
犬 ✕	犯 ✕	状 ✕	狂 ✕	狃
The 94th Radical KEN. *Inu*. A dog.	HAN. *Okasu*. To offend, transgress.	JŌ. *Katachi, sugata, fumi*. Form, appearance, condition, circumstance, a letter, written statement.	KIŌ. *Kichigai, kurū, monogurui, midareru*. To be mad, lunatic, disordered.	CHŪ. *Nareru*. To be accustomed to, familiar.
狄	狐 ✕	狎	狗 ✕	狡
TEKI. *Ebisu*. A barbarian.	KO. *Kitsune*. A fox.	KŌ. *Nareru, anadoru*. To be accustomed to, familiar, to slight, despise.	KU. *Inu*. A dog.	KŌ. *Waka-inu, warugashikoi*. A pup, cunning, knavish.
狢	狩 ✕	狹 ✕	狸 ✕	狼 ✕
KAKU. *Mujina*. An animal resembling a fox.	SHŪ, SHU. *Karu*. To hunt.	KIŌ. *Semai*. Narrow, small.	RI. *Tanuki*. A badger.	RAI. *Ōkami, urotaeru*. An animal like a wolf, embarrassed, thrown into confusion.

猥 Rō. Ōkame. A wolf, cruel.	猖 Shō. Takei, kurū. Fierce, mad, violent.	猜 Sai. Utagau, utaguru, sonemu. To doubt, suspect, envy.	猝 Sotsu. Niwaka ni. Suddenly.	猛 Mō. Takei, isamu. Fierce, strong, bold, violent.	
猥 Wai. Midari ni. Disorderly, confused, improper.	猩 Shō. — The orang-outang.	猪 Cho. Inoshishi. A wild boar, hog.	猫 Biō, Miō. Neko. A cat.	猬 I. Keharinezumi. A hedgehog, porcupine.	
猶 Yū. Beshi, nao, gotoshi. Ought, still more, again, like.	猾 Katsu. Warugashikoi, midareru. Cunning, knavish, disorderly.	猿 En. Saru. A monkey.	獄 Goku. Hitoya, uttae. A jail, complaint, criminal case.	獅 Shi. Shishi. A lion.	
獨 Doku. Hitori. Alone.	獲 Kwaku. Eru, emono. To get, game.	獵 Riō. Karu. To hunt.	獸 Jū. Kedamono. An animal.	獺 Datsu. Kawaoso. An otter.	
獻 Ken. Tatematsuru. To offer or present to a superior.					
玄 (The 95th Radical) Gen. Kuroi. Black, dark.	玆 Ji. Koko ni, kore, kono. Here, this.	率 Shutsu, ritsu. Suberu, nori, subete, shitagau, hikiyuru. To control, rules, generally, to follow, obey, lead.			玄

玉	王	玩	珊	玳
(The 96th Radical) GIOKU. Tama. A gem, precious stone, precious, Imperial.	Ō. Kimi, ōgimi. A king, sovereign, monarch.	GWAN. Moteasobu, tawamureru. To play with, sport, toy.	SAN. — Coral. 丨瑚 (San-go).	TAI. — Tortoise-shell. 丨瑁 (Tai-mai).
玻	珍	珠	班	現
HA. Mizutama. Glass, crystal. 丨璃 (Ha-ri).	CHIN. Mezurashii, takara, tattoi. Strange, rare, curious, treasure, precious.	SHU. Kai no tama. A pearl.	HAN. Wakatsu, amaneku, tsuizuru, ataeru. To divide, everywhere, to arrange in order, rank, to bestow.	GEN. Tama no hikari, arawareru. The glitter of jewels, now, to be made known.
琉	球	理	琢	琵
RIŪ. — An emerald.	KIŪ. Tama. A precious stone.	RI. Mokume, michi, kotowari, osameru. The veins in wood, reason, right, principle, nature, meaning, to govern, control.	TAKU. Migaku To polish.	BI. — A Japanese musical instrument of four strings, a lute, guitar. 丨琶 (Bi-wa).
瑕	琴	瑞	瑟	瑣
KA. Kizu. A crack, flaw.	KIN. Koto. A Japanese musical instrument, a harp, lyre.	ZUI. Shirushi no tama, saiwai. A favourable sign, happy.	SHITSU. Koto, samushii. A large lute, retired.	SA. Komaka, chiisai. Fragments, minute, small, petty.
瑠	瑳	瑾	璧	璽
RU. — Glazed pottery, an emerald. 丨璃 (Ru-ri).	SA. Migaku, uruwashii. To polish, beautiful.	KIN. Yoi tama. A fine stone.	HEKI. Tama. A precious stone, an ancient jade badge of office.	JI. Shirushi, oshite. The Imperial Seal.
環				
KWAN. Tamaki, meguru. A bracelet, ring, to go round.				

瓜	瓢				
(The 97th Radical) KWA. Uri. A melon.	HIŌ. Hisago, fukube. A gourd.				

瓦	瓶	甍	甌		
(The 98th Radical) GWA. Kawara. A tile.	HEI. Kame, modai. A jar, vase, bottle.	BŌ. Iraka. A tiled roof.	O. Kame, modai. A jar, bowl.		

甘	甚				
(The 99th Radical) KAN. Amai. Sweet.	JIN. Hanahada. Very.				

生	産	甥			
(The 100th Radical) SEI, SHŌ. Umu, ikiru, ki, nama, sugiwai, so¹ateru. To bear, live, raw, livelihood, to bring up.	SAN. Umareru, umu, nariwai. Birth, production, livelihood.	SEI. Oi. A nephew, cousin.			

用	甫				
(The 101st Radical) YŌ. Mochiiru. To use, business, use.	HO. Hajime, tasukeru. The beginning, to assist.				

田	由	甲	申	男	
(The 102nd Radical) DEN. Ta. A field, rice field, lands.	YŪ. Yoru, yoshi, nao, gotoshi, mochiiru. Subject to, on account of, cause, subject, to use, still, like, to follow.	KŌ, KATSU. Kinoe, hajime, yoroi, masaru. The first of the ten calendar signs, No. 1, A, armour, to excel.	SHIN. Mōsu, noberu, saru. To say, state, the "monkey" the 9th the twelve horary characters.	DAN, NAN. Otoko, onoko. A man, the fifth order of the nobility, a baron.	

町 Chō. Machi. A street, town, ward, measure of length and land, 3,000 tsubos.	畏 I. Osoreru, kashikomu, kashikomaru. To fear, regard with awe, squat down, assent to.	界 Kai. Sakai, kagiru. Boundary, confines, to limit.	畔 Han. Kuro, aze, hotori, somuku. A ridge or path between fields, boundary, vicinity, to disobey.	畜 Chiku. Kau, takuwau, yashinau. To keep, rear, store up, domestic animals.
留 Riū, Ru. Todomaru, tomeru. To stop, remain.	畝 Hō. Se, une. A measure of land, 30 tsubos, a ridge between fields.	畢 Hitsu. Owari, mina. The end, all.	畠 — Hatake. A field, vegetable garden.	略 Riaku. Habuku, hobo, kasumetoru, hakarigoto. To curtail, abridge, for the most part, to take by force, a plan.
畦 Kei. Une. A ridge between fields, field.	番 Han, Ban. Tsugi, tsugai. Next, a pair, turn, watch, duty, number.	畫 Gwa, Kwaku. Hakarigoto, kagiri, e, egaku. A plan, limit, picture, to draw.	異 I. Kotonaru, ayashimu, mare. To differ, consider strange, rare, foreign.	當 Tō. Ataru, masa ni, beshi, kono. To strike against, reach, happen, agree with, just, exactly, suitable, right, this.
畷 Tetsu. Nawate. A road through rice fields.	畿 Ki. Kagiri, shikimi. Limit, thresh-hold, Imperial domain.	疊 Jō. Kasaneru, tatamu, tatami. To pile up, repeat, increase, fold up, a mat.		
疋 (The 103rd Radical) Sho. Ashi, hiki. A foot, numeral for pieces of cloth, &c.	疏 So. Tōru, utoi, arai, mabara. 疎 To pass through, distant, slow, lax, coarse, sparse, open.	疑 Gi. Utagau, madou. To doubt, suspect, be bewildered.		
疒 (The 104th Radical) Taku. Yamai. A disease.	疝 Sen. — Pains or diseases in the loins or pelvic region.	疚 Kiū. Yamai, yamashii. A disease, unhealthy.	疫 Yaku, Eki. Eyami, hayariyamai. A pestilence, epidemic.	疲 Hi. Tsukare. Fatigue, exhaustion.

症 Shō. — The nature or cause of disease, a chronic malady.	疵 Shi. Kizu, yamai. A wound, scab, disease.	疽 Sho, so. Haremono. A sore, cancer, carbuncle.	疼 Tō. Itami, uzuku. Pain, to ache.	疹 Chin. — Measles, eruptions, rash.
疱 Hō. Mogasa. Small-pox.	疾 Shitsu. Sumiyaka, yamai, nikumu. Quick, a disease, to hate.	病 Biō. Yamai. Disease, sickness.	痍 I. Kasa, kizu, itamu. A sore, wound, syphilis, to hurt.	痒 Yō. Kayui. Itchy.
痔 Ji. Shiri no yamai. Piles.	痕 Kon. Ato. Remains, a scar.	痘 Tō. Mogasa. Small-pox.	痣 Shi. Hokuro. A freckle, mole.	痞 Hi. Tsukaeru. To be obstructed, constipated.
痛 Tsū, Tō. Itamu, kizutsuku. To hurt, wound.	癌 A. Oshi, ōshi. Dumb, deaf and dumb.	痲 Rin. Shibayubari. Gonorrhœa.	痴 Chi. Oroka, tsutanai. Foolish, stupid.	痰 I. Naeru, shibireru. To be numb, infirm.
痼 Ko. Nagayamai. A chronic disease.	痰 Tan. Kasuhaki. Phlegm, mucus.	瘋 Fū. Atama no yamai. Brain disease, madness.	瘖 In, on. Oshi, ōshi. Dumb, deaf and dumb.	瘡 Sō. Kasa. A boil, sore, syphilis.
瘠 Shiki. Yaseru. To be emaciated, barren.	瘍 Yō. Kizutsuku, atama no kaga. To wound, a sore head.	瘤 Riū. Kobu, hareru. A wen, tumour, to swell.	瘦 Shū. Yaseru. To be emaciated, barren.	瘧 Giaku. Okori. Ague.

(90)

痾 A. *Yamai.* Disease, illness.	療 Riō. *Iyasu.* To heal.	瘰 Rui. — Scrofula.	癈 Hai. *Sutareyamai.* An incurable disease.	癇 Kan. *Kodomo no yamai.* Convulsions in children, epileptic fits, irritability.
痨 Rō. *Itamu.* To hurt, consumption.	癖 Heki. *Kuse, tsukaeru.* A morbid tendency, indigestion, costiveness.	癨 Kwaku. *Agekudashi no yamai.* Cholera.	瘧 Shaku. — A disease of women, hysteria.	癩 Rai. *Hatake.* Leprosy.
癬 Sen. *Zenigasa, shitsu.* Ring-worm, a scrofulous sore.	癰 Yō. *Hareru, ashii dekimono.* To swell, a malignant boil.	癲 Ten. *Monogurui.* Madness.		

癶 (The 105th Radical)

癶 Hatsu. *Yuku.* To go.	癸 Ki. *Mizunoto.* The last of the ten calendar signs.	登 Tō. *Noboru, nobosu, minoru, toru.* To ascend, rise, complete, register, emboss, record, ripen.	發 Hatsu, Hotsu. *Okoru, hiraku, hanatsu.* To start, send out, rouse, open, let go, appear, a discharge of guns, &c.	

白 (The 106th Radical)

白 Haku. *Shiroi, mōsu.* White, pure, to state, make clear.	百 Hiaku. *Momo.* A hundred.	的 Teki. *Mato, akiraka.* A target, clear, bright, of (used as a postposition or particle).	皆 Kai. *Mina, tomo ni.* All, together.	皇 Kwō, Ō. *Kimi, suberagi, akiraka.* An Emperor, Sovereign, bright, exalted.
皎 Kō. *Akiraka, shiroi.* Clear, bright, white.	皓 Kō. *Akiraka, shiroi.* Clear, bright, white.	皚 Ki, Gai. *Akiraka, shiroi.* Clear, bright, white.		

(91)

皮 ✗	皴	皺	皸		皮
(The 107th Radical) Hɪ. Kawa.	Shun. Hibi, shiwa.	Shū. Shiwa.	Kun. Akagire.		
Skin, leather, bark.	Chaps produced by cold, wrinkles.	A wrinkle.	Chaps or cracks produced by cold.		

皿 ✗	盃 ✗	盆 ✗	盈 ✗	益 ✗	皿
(The 108th Radical) Bei, Myō. Sara.	Hai. Sakazuki.	Bon. Hodogi.	Ei. Michiru.	Eki. Masu, susumu, oi.	
A plate, saucer, dish.	A wine cup, glass, a cupful, full, everywhere.	A tray, pot.	To be full, complete.	More and more, many, profit, benefit, use.	

盍 ✗	盛 ✗	盜 ✗	盞 ✗	盟 ✗
Kō. Ou, nanzo.	Sei. Sakan, moru.	Tō. Nusumu, nusubito.	San. Sakazuki.	Mei. Chikau.
To cover, how? why?	Flourishing, to fill up, heap up, abundant.	To steal, a thief.	A wine cup, cup.	To take an oath, make a compact, alliance.

盡 ✗	監 ✗	蓋 ✗	盤 ✗	盥
Jin. Tsukiru, tsukusu, kotogotoku.	Kan. Miru, kangumiru, suberu.	Kai. Kedashi, ōu.	Han. Tarai, sara, tanoshimu, meguru.	Kwan. Tarai, arau.
To use up, exhaust, all.	To look at, examine, govern, control, oversee, inspect.	A word introducing a note or explanation, 蓋 for, then, now, to cover.	A basin, dish, to rejoice, wind round.	A wash-hand basin, to wash.

目 ✗	盲 ✗	直 ✗	相 ✗	盾 ✗	目
(The 109th Radical) Moku. Me, nazukeru, miru.	Mō, bō. Meshii, mekura. Blind.	Choku, jiki. Sugu, sunao, tadashii, naosu, ne.	Shō, sō. Ai, miru.	Jun. Tate. A shield.	
The eye, a square on a checker-board, to name, view.		At once, direct, honest, right, to mend, value.	Together, mutual, to look at, appearance, probability, the Premier, leading minister.		

省 ✗	眇	眜	眉 ✗	看 ✗
Shō, sei. Kaerimiru, habuku, tsukasa.	Byō. Sugame.	Bō. Kurai, kasumu.	Bi. Mayu.	Kan. Miru.
To look back, consider, diminish, reduce, Government Department, office.	Squint-eyed.	Dark, to be hazy, dim.	The eyebrows.	To see, look at, look after.

眞 ✗	眠 ✗	眤	眥	眩
Shin.	Min.	Jitsu.	Sai, shi.	Gen.
Makoto.	Nemuru.	Chikazuku.	Manajiri, maga-shira.	Mekurumeku.
Real, genuine, true.	To sleep, be drowsy.	To draw near, associate with. 眥	The corner of the eye. 眦	To be dizzy.
眷	眺 ✗	眼 ✗	睛	睡 ✗
Ken.	Chō.	Gan.	Sei.	Sui.
Kaerimiru, tagui.	Nagameru, miru.	Manako.	Hitomi.	Nemuru.
To look back, consider, be fond of, kind to, the members of one's family.	To view, gaze at.	The eye.	The pupil of the eye.	To sleep, be drowsy.
督 ✗	睦 ✗	睫	瞑	瞞
Toku.	Boku.	Shō.	Mei.	Man.
Ikiyuru, tadasu.	Mutsumajii, yawa-rageru.	Matsuge.	Mekurumeku, ne-muru, me fusagaru.	Damasu.
To lead, command, oversee, inquire into, correct.	Friendly, amicable, to soften, harmonize.	The eye-lashes.	To be giddy, drowsy, close the eyes.	To deceive.
瞥	瞭	瞚	瞬 ✗	瞻
Betsu.	Riō.	Jun.	Shun.	Sen.
Miru.	Akiraka.	Majirogu.	Matataku.	Miru.
To look at, look at for an instant, glance at.	Clear, bright.	To wink, blink.	To wink, twinkle.	To see, look at, look up.
曖	瞽			
Ai.	Ko.			
Kakureru.	Meshii, mekura.			
To hide, obscured.	A blind person.			
矛	矜			
The 110th Radical) Mō, bō, mu. Hoko.	Kiō. Hokoru, awaremu.			
A spear.	To be proud, pity.			

矢	矣	知	矧	矩
(The 111th Radical) SHI. Ya. An arrow, dart.	I. — A particle used to conclude a sentence.	CHI. Shiru, satoru, tsukasadoru. To know, perceive, acquainted with.	SHIN. Iwanya, mashite. Much more.	KU. Nori, magarigane. Dimensions, a carpenter's square, a rule.
短	矮	矯		
TAN. Mijikai, ayamachi. Short, shortcomings.	WAI. Take hikui, mijikai. Short of stature, short.	KIŌ. Tameru, itsuwaru. To straighten, rectify, to pretend.		

石	砂	砌	砥	砒
(The 112th Radical) SEKI. Ishi. A stone.	SA, SHA. Suna. Sand.	SEI. Ishidatami, migiri. A stone pavement or wall, time, period, opportunity.	SHI. Toishi. A whetstone.	HI. — Arsenic.
砦	砧	砲	破	研
SAI. Toride. A fortified place, stockade.	CHIN. Kinuta. The block used in fulling cloth, a block, anvil. 碪	HŌ. Ōzutsu. A gun, cannon.	HA. Yaburu, kudaku. To tear, break, destroy.	KEN. Migaku, suru. To polish, rub.
硫	硬	硝	硯	碇
RIŪ. Iwō. Sulphur.	KŌ. Katai. Hard.	SHŌ. Shio no neri ishi. Saltpetre.	KEN. Suzuri. An inkstone.	TEI. Ikari. An anchor.
碁	碌	碍	碎	碓
KI. Go. Chess.	ROKU. Koishi. Small stones.	GAI, GE. Samatage, sawari. Obstruction, hindrance, interruption, objection.	SAI. Kudaku. To break in pieces.	TAI. Ishiusu, usu. A stone mortar, mortar.

碑	碧	碩	磁	磊
Hi.	Heki.	Seki.	Ji.	Rai.
Ishibumi.	*Midori.*	*Ōi naru.*	*Harisuiishi.*	*Ōku no ishi, nukinjiru.*
A stone tablet, monument.	Blue, green.	Great, large, eminent.	A loadstone, stoneware.	Many stones, to excel.

磅	磋	磐	磔	磨
Hō.	Sa.	Han.	Taku.	Ma.
Ishi no koe.	*Migaku.*	*Iwa.*	*Haritsuke.*	*Togu, migaku.*
The sound of stones falling, used as a sign for a pound sterling or avoirdupois.	To polish.	A rock.	Crucifixion.	To polish, sharpen.

磬	磯	確	礎	礁
Kei.	Ki.	Kaku.	So.	Shō.
Narimono.	*Iso.*	*Katai, tashika.*	*Ishizue.*	*Iwa, kakure-iwa.*
A gong.	The sea-shore.	Hard, certain, indeed.	A stone pedestal.	A rock, a hidden rock.

礫	礦	礙	礪	
Reki.	Kwō.	Gai, ge.	Rei.	
Koishi, tsubute.	*Aragane.*	*Samatage, sawari.*	*To-ishi, arato.*	
A small stone, pebble.	Raw metal.	Obstruction, hindrance, interruption, objection.	A whetstone.	

示	社	祀	祈	祉
(The 113th Radical) Shi. *Shimesu.*	Sha. *Yashiro, nakama.*	Shi. *Matsuri, yashiro.*	Ki. *Inoru, tsugeru.*	Shi. *Saiwai, yorokobu.*
To show, inform, publish, instruct.	An altar to the spirits of the land, a Shinto shrine, company, association.	A religious celebration, fete, a Shinto shrine, a year.	To pray, petition.	Happiness, to rejoice.

祓	祝	祖	祐	神
Futsu.	Shū, shuku.	So.	Yū.	Shin, jin.
Harai.	*Notto, hafuri, iwai.*	*Hajime, moto, michi no matsuri.*	*Tasukeru, sukeru.*	*Kami, tamashii.*
Shinto prayers.	Shinto prayers, a Shinto priest, to congratulate, celebrate.	An ancestor, beginning, origin, a fete by the wayside.	To assist.	The gods, God, a spirit.

崇 Sui. Tatari. A curse, calamity, to adore.	祠 Shi. Matsuru, hokora. To worship, a Shinto shrine.	祭 Sai. Matsuri. A religious celebration, fete.	祥 Shō. Saiwai, saga. Happiness, an omen.	禄 Roku. Tamamono, saiwai. Appointment, salary, rations, happiness.
禁 Kin. Yameru, todomeru, imashimeru. To stop, forbid, prohibit.	禍 Kwa. Wazawai, sokonau. Misfortune, misery, to harm.	福 Fuku. Saiwai. Happiness, blessing.	禦 Gio. Fusegu, todomeru, kobamu. To protect, defend, ward off, stop.	禪 Zen. Yurusu. To yield, resign, the Zen Sect of Buddhists, Buddhists.
禧 Ki. Saiwai. Happiness, joy.	禮 Rei. Nori. Politeness, ceremony, thanks, acknowledgment.	禱 Tō. Inoru. To pray.		
肉 (The 114th Radical) Jū. Ashiato. A foot-print.	禽 Kin. Tori. Birds.			
禾 (The 115th Radical) Kwa. Ine, nae, awa. Grain, rice, crops.	禿 Toku. Hageru, kaburo. To be bald, bare, a young girl.	秀 Shū. Hiideru, uruwashii. To be luxuriant, beautiful, excellent.	私 Shi. Watakushi, hisoka. I, selfish, private, secret.	秋 Shū. Aki. Autumn.
科 Kwa. Shina. A branch (of study), kind, degree, series.	秒 Biō. Sukoshi. A little, a second.	秕 Hi. Shiina. An imperfect ear (of grain).	秘 Hi. Himeru. To conceal.	租 So. Mitsugi, jimen no mitsugi. Tax, duty, tribute, land tax.

秣	秤	秩	移	稀
Batsu.	Tei.	Chitsu.	I.	Ki.
Magusa.	*Hakaru.*	*Tsune, tsuizuru.*	*Utsuru, kawaru.*	*Mare.*
Fodder, grass.	To weigh.	Ordinary, fixed, order, to arrange in order.	To remove, change.	Scarce, rare, few.
税	程	稍	稔	稟
Zei.	Tei.	Shō.	Shin.	Rin, hin.
Mitsugi.	*Hodo, nori, kagiri.*	*Yaya.*	*Toshi, minoru.*	*Tamawaru, ukeru*
A tax, tribute, duties, tariff.	Extent, distance, limit.	Gradually.	A year, to ripen.	A grant from a public granary, to present to or receive from (a superior).
稜	稠	稗	種	稱
Riō.	Chū.	Hai.	Shu.	Shō.
Kado, izu.	*Shigei.*	*Hie.*	*Tane, kusagusa.*	*Tonaeru, homeru*
A corner, majesty.	Thick, dense.	A coarse kind of millet.	A seed, various kinds, sorts.	To recite, name, praise
稚	穭	稻	稼	稽
Chi.	Rei.	Tō.	Ka.	Kei.
Wakaine, itokenai.	*Kuroi, moromoro.*	*Ine.*	*Kasegu, ueru.*	*Kangaeru, osameru.*
Paddy, young.	Black, numerous.	Rice in the paddy.	To work diligently, labour, plant.	To consider, bow, study store up.
稿	稷	穀	積	穎
Kō.	Shoku.	Koku.	Seki.	Ei.
Shitagaki, inaguki, wara.	*Ine no kami.*	*Tanatsumono, yoi.*	*Tsumoru, tsumori.*	*Nogisaki, inabo, satoi.*
A draft (of a letter &c.), rice stubble, straw.	Gods of the land and grain.	Grain, cereals, good.	To heap up, accumulate, intention.	An ear of grain, clever intelligent, sharp pointed.
穗	穡	穢	穩	穫
Sui.	Shoku.	Kwai, e.	On.	Kwaku.
Ho.	*Kariosameru.*	*Kegareru, kegarawashii.*	*Odayaka.*	*Karu.*
An ear (of grain).	To reap, gather in the grain.	To be defiled, unclean.	Quiet.	To reap.

穠 Jō. *Ōi, yutaka.* Abundant, fertile.					
穴 (The 116th Radical) KETSU. *Ana.* A cave, hole.	究 Kiū. *Kiwameru.* To investigate carefully, examine judicially, be in extremities.	空 Kū. *Sora, munashii.* The sky, empty.	穽 SEI. *Otoshiana.* A pit-fall.	突 TOTSU. *Tsuku, niwaka.* To strike against, sudden.	穴
穿 SEN. *Ugatsu, horu.* To dig, pry into, penetrate, wear.	窒 CHITSU. *Fusagu.* To stop up, obstruct, nitrogen.	窘 KIN. *Kurushimu, tashinamu.* To be afflicted, in pain, to find fault with.	窟 KUTSU. *Iwaya, ana.* A cave, hole.	窪 A. *Kubomu.* To be hollow.	
窮 Kiū. *Kiwamaru.* To be in extremities, poor, exhausted, at one's wits end.	窓 Sō. *Mado.* A window. 窻	窶 RŌ. *Yatsuyatsushii.* Poor, wretched, dirty and ragged.	窺 KI. *Ukagau.* To enquire, spy out.	竄 SAN, ZAN. *Nigeru, kakureru, hanatsu.* To run away, hide, let go.	
竈 Sō. *Kamado.* A furnace.	竊 SETSU. *Nusumu, hisoka ni.* To steal, secretly, privately. 窃				
立 (The 117th Radical) RITSU, RIŪ. *Tatsu.* To stand.	竝 HEI. *Narabu, narabi, tomo ni.* To be arranged in a row, together with, unitedly, and, also.	竟 KEI, KIŌ. *Tsui ni, owaru, kiwamaru.* Finally, to finish, exhaust.	章 SHŌ. *Akiraka, aya, nori, tamazusa.* Clear, an ornament, a rule, letter, chapter, section.	竢 SHI. *Matsu.* To wait.	立

竣 SHUN. Owaru, yameru. To finish, stop.	童 DŌ. Warabe. A child.	竪 JU. Tate, shimobe. The height, length, perpendicular, a servant.	靖 SEI. Shizuka, yasui. Quiet.	竭 KETSU. Tsukiru, tsukusu. To end, exhaust.
端 TAN. Itoguchi, hashi, kiz'shi, tadashii. The beginning, origin, cause, end of a thread, edge, upright, margin, a fragment.	競 KEI, KIŌ. Kisou. To contend, compete, race.			
竹 (The 118th Radical) CHIKU. Take. Bamboo.	竺 JIKU. Take. Bamboo, India.	竿 KAN. Sao. A bamboo pole.	笄 KEI. Kōgai, kanzashi. An ornament for the hair, hairpin.	笈 KIŌ. Oi. A knapsack.
笊 SŌ. Zaru. A basket.	笑 SHŌ. Warau, emu. To laugh, smile.	笏 KOTSU, SHAKU. — A tablet carried by nobles in the presence of the Emperor.	笛 TEKI. Fue. A whistle.	笙 SHŌ. Fukimono. The name of a wind instrument, a 簫 pipe.
笞 CHI. Muchi, muchi-utsu. A whip, to whip.	笠 RITSU. Kasa. A hat, head covering.	笥 SHI. Hako. A box, hamper.	符 FU. Warifu, shirushi, awaseru. Part of a seal, a tally, sign, to unite, correspond with.	笹 — Sasa. Bamboo grass.
筏 BATSU. Ikada. A raft.	第 DAI, TEI. Tsuizuru, ie. Order, number, degree, series, a house.	筆 HITSU. Fude. A pen.	筈 KWATSU. Yahazu, hazu. The notch in an arrow, should, ought.	等 TŌ. Shina, tagui, hitoshii, ra. Quality, sort, like, a sign of the plural.

筋 **KIN.** *Suji.* A sinew, line, the authorities concerned.	筍 **JUN.** *Take-no-ko.* Bamboo sprouts. 笋	筐 **KIŌ.** *Hako.* A basket.	筒 **TŌ.** *Tsutsu.* A tube, funnel, pipe.	答 **TŌ.** *Kotaeru.* To reply.
策 **SAKU.** *Hikaru, hakarigoto, muchi.* To plan, a scheme, whip.	筧 **KEN.** *Kakehi.* A conduit pipe.	筭 **SAN.** *Kazoeru, kazu.* To calculate, count, number, arithmetic. 算	筮 **ZEI.** *Medogi.* Divining sticks.	筵 **EN.** *Takamushiro, mushiro.* A bamboo mat, a mat.
箝 **KEN.** *Hameru.* To put on, fasten, gag, forbid.	箋 **SEN.** *Fuda.* A ticket, tablet, document.	箚 **SATSU.** *Sasu, shirusu.* To prick, write down, a commission, to be stationed at (as an ambassador).	菌 **KIN.** *Kusabira.* A mushroom, toadstool.	箒 **SŌ.** *Hōki.* A broom.
管 **KWAN.** *Kuda, tsukasadoru.* A pipe, to govern, have jurisdiction over.	箭 **SEN.** *Ya.* An arrow.	箔 **HAKU.** *Sudare.* Foil (of metal), a blind made of split bamboos.	箕 **KI.** *Mi, chiritori.* A basket used for cleaning rice, a dust pan.	箱 **SŌ.** *Hako.* A box.
箴 **SHIN.** *Imashime, harisasu.* Warning, rebuke, to prick with a needle.	節 **SETSU.** *Fushi, misao.* A joint, chastity, a point or period of time.	箇 **KA, KO.** *Kazu.* A classifier of very wide application used for persons, things, places, &c. 個	範 **HAN.** *Nori, nottoru.* A law, rule, to imitate.	篆 **TEN.** — The seal character.
篇 **HEN.** *Amu, atsumeru.* A book, section, page.	築 **CHIKU.** *Kizuku, tsuku.* To construct, build.	篡 **SAN.** *Ubau.* To take by force, rob.	篝 **KŌ.** *Kagari.* A beacon.	篤 **TOKU.** *Atsui.* Kind, liberal, great.

篦	篩	簀	簇	簑
HEI.	SHI.	SAKU.	ZOKU.	SA.
Hera.	*Furui.*	*Sunoko.*	*Muragaru.*	*Mino.*
A broad thin knife, trowel.	A sieve.	Bamboo matting, a bamboo bench.	To flock together, a crowd, group.	A rain coat.
簟	簡	簣	簸	簾
TEN.	KAN.	KI.	HA.	REN.
Takamushiro.	*Fuda, tsuzumayaka.*	*Ajika, mokkō.*	*Hiru.*	*Sudare.*
A bamboo mat.	A bamboo ticket, epistle, frugal, to abridge, condense.	A basket used for carrying earth &c.	To winnow.	A blind made of thin strips of bamboo.
簿	籃	籌	籍	簪
BO.	RAN.	CHŪ.	SEKI.	SHIN.
Fuda.	*Kago.*	*Hakarigoto.*	*Fumi, fuda.*	*Kanzashi.*
A ticket, register book, account-book.	A basket.	A plan, scheme.	A book, register.	A hairpin worn as an ornament.
籐	纂	籠	籤	籬
TŌ.	SAN.	RŌ.	SEN.	RI.
Nigatake.	*Atsumeru, kumu.*	*Kago, komeru.*	*Kuji, fuda.*	*Magaki.*
Rattan.	To gather, compile, knit together.	A basket, cage, to put in.	A lot, chance, ticket.	A fence.
米 (The 119th Radical)	粉	粒	粕	粗
BEI, MAI.	FUN.	RIŌ.	HAKU.	SO.
Kome, yone.	*Kome no ko, o shiroi.*	*Tsubu.*	*Kasu.*	*Arai, hobo.*
Rice.	Rice flour, face powder, powder.	A grain of rice, pill, the numeral employed for small round objects.	Dregs.	Coarse, rough, for the most part.
粘	粟	粥	粧	粲
NEN.	ZOKU.	JUKU.	SŌ, SHŌ.	SAN.
Neyasu, nebaritsuku.	*Awa.*	*Kayu.*	*Yosoou.*	*Shiragegome, azayaka, akiraka.*
To knead, stick, be sticky.	Millet, rice in husk.	Rice gruel.	To adorn.	Washed rice, bright, glossy, clear.

粹 ✕ Sui. Kuwashii, tadashii. Minute, pure.	**精** ✕ Sei. Tadashii, yoi, shirayeru, kuwashii. Upright, sure, good, to whiten, minute, expert.	**糊** ✕ Ko. Nori. Paste.	**糖** ✕ Tō. Ame, satō. A sweet jelly made of wheat flour, sugar.	**糗** ✕ Kiū. Hoshii, irigome. Dried or cooked rice or other grain.
糞 Fun. Kuso. Dung.	**糟** Sō. Kasu, nuka. Dregs, rice bran.	**糠** Kō. Nuka. Rice bran, chaff.	**糧** Riō, Rō. Kate. Provisions, rations. 粮	**糴** Teki. Kaiyone. To buy grain.
糶 Chō. Uriyone. To sell grain.				
糸 ✕ (The 120th Radical) Shi. Ito. Fine thread.	**糺** ✕ Kiū. Tadasu. To enquire into, examine, judge, correct. 糾	**系** ✕ Kei. Ito, tsuzuku. A thread, system, line of succession, to continue.	**紀** ✕ Ki. Itosuji, shirusu. A line of threads, period of twelve years, to write down, a history, chronicle, rule, law.	**約** ✕ Yaku. Musubu, tsuzumayaka, tsuzumeru, chikau, ōmune. To bind, frugal, to restrict, an agreement, promise, generally.
紅 ✕ Kō. Kurenai, beni. Scarlet, rouge.	**紊** ✕ Bun, Bin. Midareru. Disordered, confused, in tumult.	**紃** ✕ Kiu. Azanau. To twist (a rope).	**紋** ✕ Mon. Aya. A design, crest.	**納** ✕ Nō, Tō. Ireru, osameru. To receive, collect, pay in.
紐 ✕ Chū. Himo. A cord, ribbon.	**純** ✕ Jun. Yoi, moppara. Good, pure, entirely.	**紗** ✕ Sha. Usumono. Gauze, thin silk.	**紙** ✕ Shi. Kami. Paper.	**級** ✕ Kiū. Shina, tsuide. A class, order, step, storey.

糸

紛 ナ	紜 ナ	素 ナ	紡 ナ	索
Fun.	Un.	Sō.	Hō, Bō.	Saku.
Midareru, magirawashii.	Magireru, midareru.	Shiroi, moto, sunao.	Tsumugu.	Nawa, sagasu.
Confused, perplexed, disorderly, ambiguous.	To be in confusion, ravelled.	White, origin, simple, idle.	To spin.	A rope, to search, investigate.
紫 ナ	紬	細 ナ	紳 ナ	累 ナ
Shi.	Chū.	Sai.	Shin.	Rui.
Murasaki.	Tsumugi.	Hosoi, komaka.	Ō-obi.	Kasaneru, kakaru.
Purple.	Pongee.	Thin, minute, small.	A large ornamental sash, gentleman.	To pile up, repeat, many to be involved in, dependent on.
紹 ナ	紺 ナ	終 ナ	組 ナ	絆
Shō.	Kon, kan.	Shū.	So.	Han.
Tsugu, tasukeru.	Fukai ai iro.	Owaru, tsui ni.	Kumu, kumi.	Hodasu, tsunagu.
To act as go-between, introduce, assist.	Dark-blue.	To end, finally.	To weave, club together, a company, league.	To fetter, tie up.
結 ナ	絶 ナ	絞	絡 ナ	給 ナ
Ketsu.	Zetsu.	Kō.	Raku.	Kiū.
Musubu, iu.	Taeru.	Shimeru, shiboru.	Ito, tsuranzru, matou.	Tamau, tasu.
To tie, bind.	To end, fail, be extinct, sever the connection, very.	To pull tight, strangle, squeeze, wring.	A thread, to connect, wrap round.	To give (to an inferior) supply.
統 ナ	絲 ナ	絨	絹 ナ	經 ナ
Tō.	Shi.	Jū.	Ken.	Kei, kiō.
Suberu, osameru.	Ito.	Hosonuno.	Kinu.	Heru, tate, nori, tsune.
To unite in one, govern.	Thread, a weight (the 10th part of a mō).	Fine cloth, woollen cloth.	Silk.	To pass through, erect a rule, law, usual.
綠 ナ	綢	綬	維 ナ	綯
Rioku.	Chū.	Ju.	I.	Tō.
Midori.	Tsutsumu, matou, shigei.	Kumi.	Tsunagu, tarenuno, kore, tamotsu.	Nau.
Green.	To drap round, dense, thick.	The ribbon attached to a seal, the art of braiding.	To tie, a curtain, this, to keep.	To twist or make a rope.

綱 †	網 †	綴 ✕	綸
Kō.	Mō.	Tei, tetsu.	Rin.
na, suberu.	Ami.	Tsuzuru, tsuzure.	Ito.
pe, to control, regulate.	A net.	To patch, spell, compose, rags.	A thread, Imperial.
綿 ✕	綻 ✕	緊	線 ✕
Men.	Ten.	Kin.	Sen.
Wata.	Hokorobu.	Kibishii, sumiyaka.	Itosuji.
Cotton.	To tear, open (as a bud).	Strict, stringent, pressing, quick.	A thread, line.
緒 ✕	緘 ✕	緯	締 ✕
Sho.	Kan.	I.	Tei.
oguchi, o.	Tojiru.	Nuki.	Musubu, shimaru, shimari.
nd of a thread, a thong.	To fasten together, bind.	The woof, transverse lines, parallels of latitude.	To tie, make tight, shut, strict, discipline.
編 ✕	緩 ✕	緬 ✕	練 ✕
Hen.	Kwan.	Men.	Ren.
Amu.	Yurui, yuruyaka.	Ito.	Neru.
ave, compose.	Loose, remiss.	Thread. 縮｜ (Chiri-men, crape).	To temper, practice, drill, train.
縞 ✕	縛 ✕	縊	縋
Kō.	Baku.	I.	Tsui.
Shima.	Shibaru.	Kubiru.	Sugaru, hakaru.
A stripe.	To tie.	To strangle.	To lean on, rely upon.
縫 ✕	縮 ✕	縦 ✕	縲
Hō.	Shuku.	Jū, shō.	Rui.
Nū.	Chijimaru.	Tate, hoshiimama, yurui.	Nawa.
To sew.	To shorten, shrink.	Erect, at will, gratis, slack.	A bond, fetter.

(101)

縷	纏	總 ✝	績 ✝	繁 ✝
Ru.	Ren.	Sō.	Seki.	Han.
Itosuji, tsumabiraka.	Musubu, motsureru.	Agemaki, fusa, kukuru, suberu.	Umu, isaoshi.	Shigei.
A thread, clear, minutely, particular.	To bind, be in confusion, entangled.	A lock of hair, tassel, all, to tie, control, govern, general.	To spin, merit.	Many, luxuriant.
繃	徽	繡	織 ✝	繕 ✝
Hō, nō.	Ki.	Shū.	Shiki, Shoku.	Zen.
Tsukaneru.	Nawa, shirushi.	Nuimono.	Oru.	Tsukurou.
To bind, tie up.	A rope, mark, emblem.	Embroidery, needle-work.	To weave.	To repair.
繩 ✝	繭	繪 ✝	繋 ✝	繰 ✝
Jō.	Ken.	Kwai.	Kei.	Sō.
Nawa, tadasu.	Mayu.	E, ejaku.	Tsunagu.	Kuru.
A rope, to adjust.	The silkworm, cocoon.	A picture, to draw.	To tie.	To reel, gin.
繹 ✝	辮	繼 ✝	續 ✝	纍
Eki.	Ben.	Kei.	Zoku, shoku.	Rui.
Tazuneru.	Matowaru, atsumeru.	Tsugu.	Tsuzuku.	Tsunagu, matou, nawa.
To enquire.	To plait, braid, a cue.	To succeed, inherit. 継	To continue.	To tie, wrap round, a rope.
纏 ✝	纜	纔 ✝	纖	纛
Ten.	Ran.	Zan.	Sen.	Tō.
Matou, tsukaneru.	Tomozuna.	Wazuka.	Hosoi, itosuji.	Hata.
To wrap round, bind.	A ship's hawser.	Little.	Fine, slender, a thread.	A banner, standard.
缶 (The 121st Radical)	缶 ✝	缺 ✝	缾	罐 ✝	罎
Fu, fū.		Ketsu.	Ka.	Kwan.	Don, tan.
Hodogi.		Kakeru.	Sukima.	Kogame.	Tokuri.
An earthen vessel.		To lack, be defective, incomplete.	A crack, opening.	A jar, canister.	A jar, bottle, capsule.

网					
网 (The 122nd Radical) Mō, Bō. *Ami*. A net.	罔 Mō, Bō. *Ami, nai*. A net, not.	詈 Rɪ. *Noru, nonoshiru*. To abuse, revile.	罪 Zaɪ. *Tsumi*. A sin, crime, punishment.	置 Chɪ. *Oku*. To put, place, except, let alone, fix.	
罰 Batsu. *Tsumi suru*. Punishment, to punish.	署 Shō. *Tsukasa, oku*. A Government office, to establish.	罵 Ba. *Noru, nonoshiru*. To abuse, revile.	罷 Hɪ. *Makaru*. To go, return, retire, die, used also in combination with other words as a mere embellishment of style.	罹 Rɪ. *Kakaru, au*. To be concerned in, meet with, trouble.	
羅 Ra. *Usumono, ami*. Gauze, a net.	羈 Kɪ. *Tazuna, hodashi*. A bridle, fetter, encumbrance.				
羊 (The 123rd Radical) Yō. *Hitsuji*. A sheep, goat.	美 Bɪ, Mɪ. *Utsukushii, uruwashii, yoi, yomisuru*. Lovely, beautiful, good, to esteem.	羞 Shū. *Haji, hajiru, susumeru*. Shame, to be ashamed, offer.	群 Gun. *Muragaru, ōi*. To flock together, congregate, numerous.	羨 Sen. *Urayamu, amaru*. To desire greatly, covet, remain over.	羊
義 Gɪ. *Nori, yoshi, yoi*. Right, justice, righteousness, good, patriotic, faithful.	羹 Kō. *Atsumono*. Soup.	羸 Ruɪ. *Tsukareru*. To be exhausted, emaciated.			
羽 (The 124th Radical) U. *Hane*. Feathers, wings.	翁 Ō. *Okina*. An old man.	翅 Shɪ. *Tsubasa*. Wings.	翌 Yoku. *Akiraka, akuru hi*. Next, following, tomorrow, clear.	習 Shū. *Narau, narai*. To learn, study, practice, custom, fashion.	羽

翠 ✕	翩	翫	翰 ✕	翳
SUI.	HEN.	GWAN.	KAN.	EI.
Midori.	Kakeru.	Narau, moteasobu, nareru.	Fude, fumi.	Kazasu, ōu.
Green.	To soar, fly about, flutter.	To learn, play with, become accustomed to.	A pen, writing, epistle.	To screen, ward off.
翼 ✕	翻 ✕	耀		
YOKU.	HON.	YŌ.		
Tsubasa, tasukeru.	Hirugaeru.	Kagayaku.		
Wings, to assist.	To turn over, change about, wave, translate.	To shine, light.		
老 ✕ (The 125th Radical) RŌ. Oi, toshiyori. Old, aged, venerable.	考 ✕ KŌ. Kangaeru, kangae. To consider, reflect, thought, opinion.	耄 MŌ, BŌ. (iboreru. To be in one's dotage.	者 ✕ SHA. Mono, wa, kono, hito. Thing, as for, this, person.	耆 KI. Toshiyori. An old man, an elder, old.
而 ✕ (The 126th Radical) JI, NI. Shikōshite, nanji. Yet, still, you.	耐 ✕ TAI. Shinogu, koraeru. To bear, endure.			
耒 ✕ (The 127th Radical) RAI. Suki. A plough.	耕 ✕ KŌ. Tagayasu. To cultivate (the fields), labour (as a farmer.)	耗 ✕ KŌ. Heru, herasu. To decrease, diminish.	耘 ✕ UN. Kusagiri. Weeding.	耡 JO. Suki, suku. A plough, to plough.
耳 ✕ (The 128th Radical) JI, NI. Mimi, nomi. An ear, only, a final particle.	耶 ✕ YA. Ka, chichi. An interrogative particle, a father.	耻 ✕ CHI. Haji. Shame, disgrace.	耽 ✕ TAN. Tanoshimu, fukeru. To enjoy (in a bad sense), be addicted to.	聊 ✕ RIŌ. Isasaka. Little, trifling.

聘 ☓	聖 ☓	聚 ☓	聞 ☓	聯 ☓
Hei.	Sei, shō.	Shū.	Bun, mon.	Ren.
Tō'i, mesu, metoru.	Hijiri, monoshiru.	Atsumeru.	Kiku.	Tsuranaru, tsuzuku, awaseru.
To enquire, summon, marry.	A sage, holy, sacred, Imperial.	To assemble.	To hear, news.	Arranged in a row, to continue, unite, make alliance with.
聰 ☓	聲 ☓	聳	職 ☓	聽 ☓
Sō.	Sei, shō.	Shō.	Shoku.	Chō, tei.
Mimitoi, satoi.	Koe, oto, hibiki, homare.	Sobieru.	Tsukasa, waza, moppara.	Kiku.
Quick of hearing, intelligent.	Voice, sound, report, praise.	To tower up.	Office, duty, trade, occupation, single, really.	To hear, listen.
聾				
Rō.				
Mimishii.				
Deaf.				
聿	肅	肇		
(The 129th Radical)	Shuku.	Chō.		
Itsu.	Tsutsushimu, kibishii.	Nagai, hajime.		
Fude.	To be respectful, reverential, severe.	Long, the beginning, intelligent.		
A pen, pencil.				
肉 ☓	肋	肌 ☓	肖 ☓	肘
The 130th Radical)	Roku.	Ki.	Shō.	Chū.
Niku.	Wakibone, abara.	Hada, hadae.	Niru, katadoru.	Hiji, kaina.
Shishi.	The ribs.	The skin, naked body.	To resemble, make in the likeness of.	The elbow, the arm between the elbow and shoulder.
Flesh, meat.				
肝	股	肢	肥 ☓	胚
Kan.	Ko.	Shi.	Hi.	Hai.
Kimo.	Momo.	Te-ashi, eda.	Koeru.	Haramu.
The liver.	The thigh.	The hands and feet, limbs.	To be fat, fertile.	To be pregnant.

聿

肉
月

肩 ✕ KEN. *Kata, masaru.* The shoulder, to excel.	肯 ✕ KŌ. *Gaenzuru.* To consent, assent.	肱 ✕ KŌ. *Hiji.* The elbow.	育 ✝ IKU. *Yashinau, sodateru.* To nourish, rear up, educate.	肺 ✕ HAI. *Fukubukushi.* The lungs.
胃 ✕ I. *Kusobukuro.* The stomach, digestion.	胄 ✕ CHŪ. *Tane, sue, tsuzuku.* Seed posterity, to continue.	背 ✕ HAI. *Senaka, ushiro, somuku.* The back, behind, to disobey.	胞 HŌ, BŌ. *kine.* The placenta, brotherly.	胎 TAI. *Haramu.* To be pregnant.
胡 ✕ KO. *Nanzo, ebisu.* How? why? a barbarian.	胤 ✕ IN. *Tane, tsuzuku, tsugu.* A seed, to continue, succeed to.	胴 ✕ DŌ. — The trunk (of a body).	胯 ✕ KO, KWA. *Matagura, matagu.* The crotch, groin, to straddle, step across.	能 ✕ NŌ. *Yoi, taeru, atau, waza.* Good, to endure, be able, skill, the name of a dance.
胸 ✕ KIŌ. *Mune.* The chest, breast, heart.	脂 SHI. *Abura.* Fat, grease, suet.	脅 ✕ KIŌ. *Waki, waki no shita, obiyakasu.* The side, arm-pit, to frighten, intimidate. 脇	脉 ✝ MIAKU. *Suji, chi no suji.* The pulse, a line, range.	脊 ✕ SEKI. *Senaka.* The back.
脆 ✕ ZEI. *Moroi.* Brittle, weak.	脚 KIAKU. *Ashi.* A foot.	脛 KEI. *Hagi.* The shin.	唇 SHIN. *Kuchibiru.* The lips.	脱 ✝ DATSU. *Monukeru, manukareru, saru, nozoku.* To cast off (as a skin), escape, leave, leave out.
腕 ✕ WAN. *Ude.* The arm.	脹 ✕ CHŌ. *Fukureru.* To swell, be inflated, puffed up, angry.	腓 HI. *Komura.* The calf of the leg.	腫 SHŌ, SHU. *Hareru.* To swell.	腐 ✝ FU. *Kusaru.* To decay, rot.

(109)

腎	脾	腰 ✕	腸 ✕	腹 ✕
Jin.	Hi.	Yō.	Chō.	Fuku.
Murato.	—	Koshi.	Harawata.	Hara.
The kidneys.	The spleen.	The loins.	The intestines.	The belly.
腦 ✕	腥	膏 ✕	肩 ✕	膜
Nō.	Sei.	Kō.	Fu.	Maku.
Nazuki.	Namigusai.	Abura, aburazuku, uruosu.	Hada, hadae.	Tanashishi.
The brain.	Smelling like raw fish or flesh.	Grease, fat, ointment, to enrich.	The skin.	A membrane.
膠	膨 ✕	膳 ✕	膰	膽 ✕
Kō.	Bō.	Zen.	Han.	Tan.
Nikawa.	Fukureru.	Sonaeru, kuimono.	Himorogi.	Kimo.
Glue.	To swell.	To prepare, eatables, a dining table.	Flesh offered in sacrifice.	The liver, gall.
膺	臀	膾	臂	膝 ✕
Yō.	Den.	Kwai.	Hi.	Shitsu.
Mune, utsu, ukeru, fusagaru, ataru.	Shiri, izarai.	Namasu.	Hiji.	Hiza.
The breast, to strike, receive, be obstructed, reach.	The buttocks, bottom.	Hash made of meat, fish, vegetables, &c.	The elbow.	The knee.
臆	膿	臟 ✕		
Oku.	Nō.	Zō.		
Mune.	Umi.	—		
The breast, heart, mind, ideas, feelings.	Pus.	The viscera. 丨腑 (Zō-fu).		
臣 ✕	臥 ✕	臨 ✕		
(The 131st Radical) Shin. Kerai.	Gwa. Fusu.	Rin. Nozomu, miru.		
A retainer, minister, officer, subject.	To lie down.	To approach, be at the point of, behold, unexpected, special.		

臣

自	自 ✕ (The 132nd Radical) JI. *Yori, mizukara, onozukara.* From, one's self, of its own accord, spontaneously.	臭 ✕ SHŪ. *Kusai.* Stinking, a smell.			
至	至 ✕ (The 133rd Radical) SHI. *Itaru.* To arrive, reach, very, as to.	到 ✕ TŌ. *Itaru.* To reach.	致 ✕ CHI. *Itasu, itaru, omomuku.* To do, finish, go, reach, convey.	臻 ✕ SON. *Shikiri ni, itaru.* Constantly, to reach.	臺 ✚ TAI, DAI. *Utena.* The calyx of a flower, a high terrace, stand.
臼	臼 ✕ (The 134th Radical) KIŪ. *Usu.* A mortar.	臾 ✕ YU. *Shibaraku.* A short time.	舁 ✕ YO. *Kaku, ageru.* To carry on the shoulders, lift up.	舂 ✕ SHŌ. *Usutsuku.* To pound in a mortar.	舅 ✕ KIŪ. *Shūto.* A father-in-law.
	與 ✕ YO. *Oyobi, to, tomoni, azukaru, kumisuru, ataeru, yori, ya, ka.* And, together, with, to take part in, join, bestow, from, an interrogative particle, interjection.	興 ✕ KIŌ, KŌ. *Okoru, okosu, sakan.* To rise, raise, prosperous, to promote.	擧 ✕ KIO. *Ageru, mina, kozoru.* To raise, lift up, a'l, to assemble.	舊 ✕ KIŪ. *Moto, furui, hisashii, mukashi.* Formerly, old, ancient, the olden times.	釁 KIN. *Hibi, kizu, chinuru.* A crack, flaw, opening, rupture of frie dly relations, to smear with blood.
舌	舌 ✚ (The 135th Radical) ZITSU. *Shita.* The tongue.	舍 ✚ SHA. *Ie, yadoru, todomaru.* A house, to lodge, stop.	舐 SHI. *Neburu, nameru.* To lick.	舒 JO. *Noberu, yuruyaka, omomuro.* To extend, softly, tranquil, remiss.	
舛	舛 (The 136th Radical) SEN. *Somuku.* To oppose.	舞 ✕ BU. *Mau.* To dance, posture.			

(111)

舟 (The 137th Radical) SHŪ. *Fune.* A boat.	航 KŌ. *Fune, funawatashi.* A boat, to cross a river or the sea, navigation.	般 HAN, HEN. *Tabi, tanoshimu.* A time, sort, way, fashion, to rejoice, transport.	船 SEN. *Fune.* A boat, ship.	舳 JIKU. *Tomo.* The stern of a boat.	舟
舵 DA. *Kaji.* A rudder.	舶 HAKU. *Ōbune, umibune.* A large boat, sea-going boat, ship.	舷 GEN. *Funabata.* The gunwale of a boat.	艀 FU. *Kobune, hashibune.* A small boat, cargo boat.	艇 TEI. *Kobune.* A small boat.	
艘 SŌ. *Fune.* The numeral for boats, ships, &c.	艙 SŌ. — The hold of a vessel.	艪 RO. — An oar, skull. 櫓	艤 GI. *Funayosoi.* The equipment of a vessel.	艦 KAN. *Ikusabune.* A man-of-war.	
艨 MŌ. *Ikusabune.* A man-of-war.	艫 RO. *Tomo.* The stern of a vessel.				
艮 (The 138th Radical) KON, GON. *Todomaru, kagiru, katai, ushi-tora.* To stop, limit, hard, the N. E.	良 RIŌ. *Yoi.* Good, excellent, skillful.	艱 KAN. *Nayamu, habamu.* To be distressed, afflicted.			艮
色 (The 139th Radical) SHOKU, SHIKI. *Iro.* Colour, sort, appearance, love, lewdness, a lover.	艶 EN. *Uruwashii, utsukushii.* Glossy, beautiful, lovely.				色

(112)

艸 ×	艾	芋	芍	芙
The 140th Radical) Sō. Kusa.	Kai, Gai. Mogusa yomogi.	U. Imo.	Shaku. Kaoyogusa.	Fu. Hachisu.
Grass.	The moxa, mugwort.	A potato.	The peony.	The lotus. 蓉 (Fu-yō).
芝 ×	芥	花 ×	芳 ×	芬 ×
Shi. Shiba.	Kai. Karashi, akuta.	Kwa. Hana.	Hō. Kōbashii.	Fun. Kōbashii.
Turf.	Mustard, rubbish.	A flower.	Fragrant.	Fragrant.
芹	芽 ×	苑	苔 ×	苗 ×
Kin. Seri.	Ga, Ge. Me. 芽	En. Sono.	Tai. Koke.	Biō. Nae.
Parsley.	A bud.	A flower garden.	Moss.	Young shoots.
苛	苞	苴	苟 ×	若 ×
Ka. Iratsu.	Hō. Tsuto.	So, Sho. Tsuto, tsutsumu.	Kō. Moshi, igashikumo, karisome ni.	Jaku. Wakai, gotoshi, moshi, nanji, shiku
To irritate.	A straw wrapper, present, bribe.	A straw wrapper, to wrap round, a bribe.	If, supposing that.	Young, like, if, you, perhaps.
苦 ×	苧	苫	英 ×	苺
Ku. Kurushimu, nigai.	Cho. O.	Sen. Toma.	Ei. Hanabusa, hiideru.	Bai. Ichigo.
To suffer pain, trouble, affliction, bitter, cruel.	Hemp.	A mat used for covering cargo, or for roofing.	A flower, to excel.	A strawberry, raspberry.
茂 ×	茄	茅	茜	茨
Mo. Shigeru.	Ka. Nasubi.	Bō. Kaya.	Shin. Akane.	Shi. Ibara.
Luxuriant, dense.	The egg-plant.	A rush.	Madder.	A prickly plant.

茲 **SHI.** *ko ni, kono.* Here, this.	茶 **SA.** *Cha.* Tea.	荊 **KEI.** *Ibara, odoro.* A bramble-bush, thicket.	草 **SŌ.** *Kusa.* Grass.
荷 **KA.** *Ninau, ni.* carry, baggage, goods, cargo.	荻 **TEKI.** *Ogi.* A reed.	莊 **SŌ.** *Ogosoka.* Stern, majestic.	莠 **YŪ.** *Hagusa.* Tares, weeds.
莖 **KEI.** *Kuki.* stem, stalk.	菩 **GAN.** *Tsubomi.* A flower bud.	莫 **BAKU.** *Nashi, nakare.* A negative, do not, have not.	菊 **KIKU.** — The Chrysanthemum.
菅 **KWAN.** *Suge.* of rush used for ting mats, &c., sedge.	菓 **KWA.** *Kudamono.* Fruit.	菖 **SHŌ.** *Ayame.* The iris.	菴 **AN.** *Iori.* A cottage.
萌 **HŌ.** *ru, kizashi.* prout, bud, the beginning, sign, tendency.	萄 **DŌ.** *Ebi.* A grape.	萎 **I.** *Shioreru, shibomu.* To wither, shut.	萬 **BAN, MAN.** *Yorozu.* Ten thousand, all, a myriad. 万
落 **RAKU.** *iru, mura.* all, be omitted, a village.	葉 **YŌ.** *Ha.* A leaf.	著 **CHAKU, CHO.** *Arawareru, ichijirushii, kiru.* To be manifest, clear, to put on, publish (as a hook), compose.	葛 **KATSU.** *Kuzu, katsura.* A creeping plant (the Polichos tuberosus).

董 Tō. Tadasu. To enquire into, judge, adjust.	葩 HA. Hanabira. The petals of a flower.	葦 I. Ashi. A large rush.	葬 Sō. Hōmuru. To bury.	葱 Sō. Negi, nebuka. An onion, a kind of garlic.
葺 Shū. Fuku. To roof, thatch.	葵 KI. Aoi. The holly-hock.	蒙 Mō. Kōmuru, ōu, kurai. To receive from a superior, cover, dark, dull.	蒜 SAN. Ninniku. Garlic.	蒲 Ho. Gama. A bulrush.
蒸 Jō. Musu. To steam, to be damp and hot (as the weather).	蒼 Sō. Aoi. Green, blue.	蓆 SEKI. Mushiro, ōi naru. A mat made of straw, large, numerous.	蓑 SA. Mino. A raincoat.	蓬 Hō. Yomogi. Mugwort. 蓬莱 (Hō-rai, Elysium).
蓮 REN. Hasu, hachisu. The lotus.	蔑 BETSU. Naigashiro ni suru. To slight, despise.	蔓 MAN. Tsuru. A vine.	蔦 CHŌ. Tsuta. Ivy.	蔬 So. Na. Greens, vegetables.
蔭 IN. Ōu, kage. To cover, shade.	蔕 TEI. Heta, hoso. Rootlets, flower-stalks, fruit-stalks, unimportant.	蔽 HEI. Ōu, kakusu. To cover, hide.	蕃 HAN. Shigeru. To be luxuriant, dense.	蕉 SHŌ. — The Banana. 芭蕉 (Ba-shō).
蕎 KIŌ. Soba. Buck-wheat.	華 KWA. Hana. A flower.	蕣 SHUN. Asagao. The convolvulus.	蕨 KETSU. Warabi. A fern.	蕩 TŌ. Torakasu, hiroi. To melt, fascinate, wide.

(115)

蕪 **Bu.** *Kabura.* A turnip.	蕾 **Rai.** *Tsubomi.* A bud.	薄 ✗ **Haku.** *Usui.* Thin, light.	薦 ✗ **Sen.** *Wara, susumeru.* Straw, to present (to a superior).
薩 ✗ **Satsu.** *Hotoke.* A Buddha.	薪 ✗ **Shin.** *Takigi.* Firewood.	薮 ✗ **Sō.** *Yabu.* A thicket, grove.	薫 **Kun.** *Kaoru.* To be fragrant.
藏 ✗ **Zō.** *ra, kakusu.* down, to hide.	藝 ✗ **Gei.** *Waza.* The arts, accomplishments.	藤 ✗ **Tō.** *Fuji.* The wistaria.	藥 ✗ **Yaku.** *Kusuri.* Medicine, powder.
藷 **Sho.** *Imo.* for plants with s, a yam, sweet potato.	藹 **Ai.** *Sakan, shigeru.* Flourishing, dense.	蘆 **Ro.** *Ashi.* A rush.	蘇 ✗ **So.** *Yomigaeru.* To rise from the dead, the name of a plant.
蘚 **Sen.** *Koke.* Moss.			
虎 ✗ **Ko.** *Tora.* A tiger.	虐 ✗ **Giaku.** *Shietageru.* To oppress, tyrannize over, treat with cruelty.	處 ✗ **Sho.** *Oru, tokoro.* To be, a place, to manage, appoint, judge.	虛 ✗ **Kio.** *Munashii, ōzora.* Empty, in vain, space.

虍

	Rio. Toriko, toraeru. A prisoner, to arrest.	Gō. Yobu, nazukeru, sakebu. A number, designation, to call, name, cry out, used as a numeral, and with the names of ships.	Gu. Omompakaru, sonaeru. To consider, be anxious about, provide.		
	虫 (he 142nd Radical) KI. Mushi, hebi. An insect, reptile.	虱 Shitsu. Shirami. A louse.	虻 Bō. Abu. A horse-fly.	虹 Kō. Niji. A rainbow.	蚓 In. Mimizu. A worm.
	蚊 Bun. Ka. A mosquito.	蚤 Sō. Nomi. A flea.	蛆 Shō. Uji. A maggot.	蛇 Ja, da. Hebi. A snake.	蛙 A. Kawazu. A frog.
	蛤 Gō. Hamaguri. A clam.	蛬 Kiō. Kirigirisu. A cricket.	蛭 Tetsu. Hiru. A leech.	蛾 Ga. Hiiru. A silkworm moth.	蜈 Go. Mukade. A centipede. | 蚣 (Go-shō).
	蜂 Hō, bō. Hachi. A bee, wasp.	蜆 Ken. Shijimi. A kind of shell fish.	蜕 Sei, zei. Monukeru. To slip out of, excel.	蜻 Sei. Tombo. A dragon fly. | 蜓 (Sei-tei).	蜘 Chi. Kumo. A spider. | 蛛 (Chi-shu).
	蜜 Mitsu. — Honey.	蝕 Shoku. Mushibamu. To be moth-eaten.	蝠 Hen. Kōmori. A bat. | 蝠 (Hem-puku).	蝶 Chō. — A butterfly.	蝸 Kwa. Katatsumuri. A snail.

(117)

蝗	融 ✗	螢 ✗	螺	蟋
Kwō.	Yū.	Kei.	Ra.	Rō.
Inamushi.	Tōru, tokeru, yawaragu.	Hotaru.	Horagai.	Kera. re.
A locust.	To circulate, melt, harmonize.	A firefly.	A conch shell.	A cricket.
蟄	蟬 ✗	蟠	蟲 ✗	螳
Chitsu.	Sen.	Han.	Chū.	Tō.
Hisomu.	Semi.	Wadakamaru.	Mushi.	Kamakiri.
To be hidden, confined, hibernate.	A cicada.	To be coiled up, winding.	Insects, worms.	A mantis. 螂 (Tō-rō).
蟹	蟻 ✗	蠅 ✗	蠢 ✗	蠟 ✗
Kai.	Gi.	Yō.	Shun.	Rō.
Kani.	Ari.	Hai.	Ugomeku.	—
A crab.	An ant.	A fly.	To crawl, wriggle, (as an insect).	Wax, enamel.
蠣	蠶 ✗	蠻 ✗		
Rei.	San.	Ban.		
Kaki.	Kaiko.	Ebisu.		
An oyster.	A silk-worm.	A barbarian.		
血 ✞	漿 ✞			
(The 143rd Radical)	Shū.			
Ketsu.	Moromoro, ōi.			
Chi.				
Blood.	All, many.			
行 ✗	衍	街	術 ✗	衢
(The 144th Radical)	En.	Gen.	Jutsu.	Gai.
Kō, Giō.	Amaru, afureru.	Terau.	Tedate, nori.	Chimata.
Yuku, aruku, okonau. To step, go, walk, act, arranged in a row.	To be superfluous, overflow, abundant, fertile.	To boast, sell one's self.	A device, trick, rule, art.	Forks in a road, cross roads, a town.

血

行

(119)

虚 ‛A, GO. Torisurigotodono. A Government office.	衛 † EI. Mamoru. To defend, protect.	衝 † SHŌ. Tsuku. To strike against.	衡 KŌ. Yokotawaru, hakarisao, kubiki. To be across, a weighing beam, yoke.	
虫	衣 † (The 145th Radical) I. Koromo. Clothing.	表 † HIŌ. Omote, arawasu. The outside, front, to disclose.	衰 † SUI. Otoroeru. To fall, degenerate.	裏 † CHŪ. Uchi, makoto. The inside, truth, equity.	衾 KIN. Fusuma. A quilt.
	袂 † BEI. Tamoto. The pocket in the sleeve of a garment.	袈裟 KE-SA. A scarf or surplice worn by Buddhist priests.	袋 † TAI. Fukuro. A bag.	袒 TAN. Katanugu. To uncover the shoulder, strip one's self to the waist.	袖 † SHŪ. Sode. A sleeve.
	被 † HI. Yoru no kimono, ōu, kōmuru, ruru. Bed clothes, to cover, receive (from a superior), the sign of the passive voice.	袴 † KO. Hakama. Loose trowsers.	袷 KŌ. Awase. A lined garment.	裁 × SAI. Tatsu, wakatsu, hakaru. To cut out (clothes), divide, discriminate, judge.	裂 † RETSU. Saku, tachiamari. To tear, remnants.
	裕 YU. Yutaka. Abundant, fertile.	裔 EI. Sue. The skirt of a robe, a border, descendants.	裡 † RI. Ura, uchi. The inside, lining.	補 † HO. Oginau, tasukeru. To supplement, restore, assist.	装 † SŌ. Yosoou, kazaru. To dress, adorn one's self.
	裨 HI. Tasukeru. To assist.	裳 × SHŌ. Mo, mosuso. The skirt of a garment.	裸 × RA. Hadaka. Naked.	裾 × KIO. Suso. The skirt of a garment.	製 × SEI. Tsukuru, tatsu. To make, manufacture, cut out (clothes).

複 **FUKU.** *Kasaneru,* To pile up, increase, repeat.	褫 **CHI.** *Nugu, ubau.* To take off, deprive of.	襃 ✕ **HŌ.** *Homeru.* To praise.	褥 **JOKU.** *Shitone.* A mattress.	褸 **RU.** *Boro, tsuzure.* Rags.
襪 **BETSU.** *Tabi.* Stockings.	襟 ✕ **KIN.** *Eri.* The collar of a garment.	襦 **JU.** *Hadagi.* A garment worn next the skin.	襲 **SHŪ.** *Osou, kasaneru, tsugu.* To attack, invade, pile up, inherit.	襷 **HAN.** *Tasuki.* A cord used for fastening up the sleeves.
囊 **NŌ.** *Fukuro.* A bag.				
襾 (The 146th Radical) **A, KA.** *Ōu.* To cover.	西 ✕ **SAI, SEI.** *Nishi.* The West.	要 ✕ **YŌ.** *Kaname, motomeru.* The rivet of a fan, essential, principal, important, necessary, to ask for.	覆 ✕ **FUKU, FU.** *Ōu, kutsugaeru.* To cover, upset, overthrow.	羈 **KI.** *Hodashi.* A fetter, shackle, encumbrance.
見 ✕ (The 147th Radical) **KEN.** *Miru.* To see.	規 ✕ **KI.** *Nori, tadasu, hakaru, bummawashi.* A law, rule, to correct, measure, compasses.	視 ✕ **SHI.** *Miru, nazoraeru.* To see, inspect, imitate.	覗 ✕ **TO.** *Miru.* To see, look at.	親 ✕ **SHIN.** *Shitashimu, oya, mizukara, chikazuku.* Friendship, affection, parents, self, to associate with.
覬 **KI.** *Negau.* To hope for.	覺 ✕ **KAKU.** *Oboeru, satoru, sameru.* To learn, discern, awake.	覽 ✕ **RAN.** *Miru.* To see look at.	觀 ✕ **KWAN.** *Miru, akiraka ni miru, shimesu.* To see, see clearly, inspect, show.	

西
見

觜 SHI. *Kuchibashi.* The bill or beak of a bird.	解 ✕ KAI, GE. *Toku, wakatsu, hodoku, wakaru.* To explain, melt, untie, cut up, disperse, understand.	觸 ✕ SHOKU. *Fure, fureru.* A notification, Government proclamation, to touch, infringe, publish.	
訂 ✕ TEI. *Tadasu.* To examine into, judge, correct.	訃 FU. *Tsugeru.* To announce (a death).	計 ✕ KEI. *Hakarigoto, hakaru, kazoeru.* A plan, to reckon, calculate, number.	信 SHIN. *Makoto, otozure.* Truth, faith, tidings, to believe.
討 ✕ TŌ. *Utsu, tazuneru.* To smite, chastise, investigate.	訣 ✕ KETSU. *Abaku.* To break open, divulge.	訓 ✕ KUN. *Oshieru, yomi.* To teach, doctrine, instruction, to follow (as instruction), the Japanese rendering of a Chinese character.	託 ✕ TAKU. *Kakotsuke, yudaneru.* Pretext, excuse, to entrust to, charge with.
訛 ✕ KWA. *Ayamari, itsuwari.* Mistake, lie.	訝 GA. *Ibukaru, negirau.* To wonder at, express surprise, meet (as a guest).	訟 ✕ SHŌ. *Uttaeru.* To accuse, bring a complaint or suit, confess.	訣 KETSU. *Wakare, wakareru.* Parting, to separate.
訪 ✕ HŌ. *Toi, tomurau.* To enquire, visit.	設 ✕ SETSU. *Mōkeru.* To earn, get, make, establish.	許 ✕ KIO. *Yurusu, moto.* Permission, pardon, to allow, house, home, you.	訴 ✕ SO. *Uttaeru.* To accuse, bring a complaint or suit against, confess.
註 CHŪ. *Shirusu, arawasu.* Commentary, notes, explanation.	詁 KO. *Oshieru.* To teach.	詎 KIO. *Nanzo, yamu.* How, why, to stop.	詐 ✕ SA. *Itsuwari.* A lie, deception, fraudulent.

詔 ✝	評 ✕	詛	詞 ✝	詠 ✝
Shō.	Hiō.	So.	Shi.	Ei.
Mikotonori.	Hakaru, sadameru, tadasu.	Norou.	Kotoba.	Uta, utayomu, nagame.u.
An Imperial edict.	To weigh, discuss the merits of, criticize, deliberate.	To curse.	A word, literary style.	To sing, compose poetry, gaze at.

詢	詣 ✝	試 ✝	詩 ✝	詫 ✕
Jun.	Kei.	Shi.	Shi.	Ta.
Tou, hakaru.	Itaru, mōderu.	Kokoromiru.	Karauta.	Wabiru.
To enquire, question, consult with.	To reach, go to a temple.	To try, examine.	Chinese poetry, a poem.	To apologize, confess, acknowledge.

詬	詭	詮 ✕	詰 ✝	話 ✝
Kō.	Ki.	Sen.	Kitsu.	Wa.
Haji, ikaru.	Azamuku.	Erabu, hakaru.	Najiru, tsumeru.	Hanasu.
Shame, disgrace, to be angry.	To deceive.	To choose, estimate, deliberate.	To enquire closely into, pack, fill, perform official duty.	To speak.

該 ✕	詳 ✕	註	誅 ✕	誂 ✕
Gai.	Shō.	Kai.	Chu.	Chō.
Mina, sono, sonaeru, kaneru.	Tsumabiraka.	Ayamari.	Semeru, korosu.	Atsuraeru, mote-asobu.
All, that, proper, to provide, comprehend.	Clear.	A mistake, misdemeanour.	To chastise, slay, punish with death.	To order, play with.

誇 ✝	誌 ✝	認 ✝	誕	誓 ✕
Kwa.	Shi.	Nin.	Kiō, kō.	Sei.
Ogoru.	Shirusu.	Mitomeru, shita-tameru.	Taburakasu.	Chikai, chikau.
To be proud, boast.	To write down, record.	To recognize, acknowledge, write.	To deceive, seduce.	An oath, promise, to swear, vow.

誕 ✝	誘 ✝	誼 ✝	語 ✕	誠 ✕
Tan.	Yū.	Gi.	Go, gio.	Sei.
Azamuku, uma-reru.	Izanau, michibiku.	Yoroshii.	Kataru.	Makoto.
To deceive, be born.	To invite, lead, seduce.	Good.	To tell, relate.	Truth, sincerely, indeed.

誡 ナ KAI. Imashimeru. To warn, admonish, commandment.	誣 FU. Shiyuru. To slander, accuse wrongfully.	誤 × GO. Ayamari. An error, mistake.	誦 ナ SHŌ. Yomu, soranjiru. To read, recite from memory.	誨 ナ KWAI. Oshieru. To teach.
說 ナ SETSU, ZEI. Toku, noberu. To explain, saying, doctrine, opinion, report.	誰 ナ SUI. Tare, taso. Who.	課 ナ KWA. Osu, hakaru. To fix, tax, a lesson, task, bureau.	誹 × HI. Soshiru. To slander, revile.	調 × CHŌ. Totonou, shiraberu. To adjust, regulate, investigate, examine, judge.
諂 ナ TEN. Hetsurau. To flatter.	諛 YU. Hetsurau. To flatter.	談 ナ DAN. Kataru. To tell, relate.	請 ナ SEI. Negau, motomeru, kou. To ask, request, beg, invite.	諍 SŌ. Isameru, arasou. To remonstrate with, strive, compete.
諏 SU. Tou, hakaru. To enquire, measure.	諒 RIŌ. Makoto, tasuke. Truth, help.	論 ナ RON. Arasou. To discuss, dispute, argument, discourse.	諜 CHŌ. Ukagau, saguru. To spy out, search.	諫 × KAN. Isameru. To remonstrate with, admonish.
諭 ナ YU. Satosu, tatoe. To make known authoritatively, instruct, a comparison.	諮 SHI. Hakaru, tou. To consult with, enquire.	諱 KI. Imina. The name a person receives at the age of fifteen, a posthumous name.	諳 ナ AN. Soranjiru. To recite from memory.	諷 FŪ. Tsugeru, satosu, soshiru. To announce indirectly, to censure indirectly.
諸 ナ SHO. Moromoro, kore, kokoni. All, various, this, here, a final particle.	諺 ナ GEN. Kotowaza. A proverb.	諾 × DAKU. Ubenau. To agree with, acquiesce.	謀 × BŌ. Hakarigoto. A plot, plan.	謁 ナ ETSU. Mamieru, mōsu. To have an audience, state.

謎	謐	謗 ✗	謙 ✗
Mei.	Hitsu.	Bō.	Ken.
Nazo.	Shizuyaka.	Soshiru.	Herikudaru.
A riddle.	Quiet.	To slander, revile.	To humble one's self.
講 ✗	謝 ✗	謠 ✗	謫
Kō.	Sha.	Yō.	Taku, teki.
tkasu, narau.	Shirizoku, wabiru.	Utau.	Togameru, tsumi suru.
:plain, practise.	To retire, thank, apologize.	To sing.	To blame, punish, banish.
謹 ✗	謄 ✗	譁	譃
Kin.	Tō.	Kwa.	Kio.
utsushimu.	Utsusu.	Kamabisushii.	Soragoto, itsuwari.
be reverential, Ircumspect.	To copy.	Noisy.	A falsehood.
譏 ✗	識 ✗	譚	譜
Ki.	Shiki.	Tan.	Fu.
Soshiru.	Shiru.	Monogatari.	Fuda, tsuzuki.
To slander.	To know.	Story, history.	Record, chronicles, a register.
警 ✗	譬	譯 ✗	議 ✗
Kei.	Hi.	Yaku.	Gi.
'oru, imashi- eru, tadasu.	Tatoeru, tatoe.	Wake, wakeru.	Hakaru, arasou.
:arm, admonish, Instruct.	To illustrate, an example, a comparison.	Reason, to explain, translate.	To debate, discuss.
護 ✗	譽 ✗	讀 ✗	讃 ✗
Go.	Yo.	Toku, doku.	San.
Mamoru.	Homeru, homare.	Yomu.	Homeru.
defend, protect.	To praise, renoun.	To read.	To praise.

變 ✕	讎 ✚	譖 ✚	讓 ✕
HEN.	SHŪ.	ZAN.	JŌ.
Kawaru.	Ada.	Soshiru.	Yuzuru.
To change, a phenomenon.	An enemy.	To slander.	To yield.

讜			
TŌ.			
Kotoba tadashii.			
Right words.			

谷 ✚	谿 ✕	豁	
(The 150th Radical)	KEI.	KWATSU.	
KOKU.	Tani.	Hogaraka, tōru.	
Tani.			
A valley.	A mountain stream, rivulet. 溪	Bright, clear, to understand thoroughly.	

豆 ✚	豈 ✕	豐 ✕	
(The 151st Radical)	KI, GAI.	HŌ, BU.	
TŌ, ZU.	Ani.	Yutaka, toyo.	
Mame.			
A bean, pea.	An introductory exclamation, how?	Fertile, abundant. 豐	

豕 ✚	豚 ✕	象 ✚	豪 ✕
(The 152nd Radical)	TON.	SHŌ, ZŌ.	GŌ.
SHI.	Buta.	Katachi, katadoru.	Sugureru, tsuyoi.
Inoko, buta.			
A pig.	A pig.	Shape, form, appearance, an elephant, to copy, imitate, make in the likeness of.	Excellent, excelling, powerful.

豸	豹	豺	貂
(The 153rd Radical)	HIŌ.	SAI.	CHŌ.
CHI.	Nagatsukami.	Yamainu.	Ten.
Ashi naki mushi, hau mushi.			
Reptiles.	A leopard.	A wolf, wild beast.	A marten, sable.

貝	貞	負	財	貢
(The 154th Radical) BAI, MAI. Kai. A shell.	TEI. Tadashii. Upright, chaste.	FU. Ou, somuku, makeru. To carry on the back, a load, duty, debt; to receive (as a wound), to disobey, lose.	SAI, ZAI. Takara. Wealth, property.	KŌ. Mitsugi. Tribute, a tax.
貧	貨	販	貪	貫
HIN. Mazushii. Poor.	KWA. Takara. Wealth, property, goods.	HAN. Hisagu. To hawk, peddle.	TAN, TON. Musaboru. To covet.	KWAN. Tsuranuku. To pierce through, connect, pervade, a string of cash.
責	貯	貳	貴	貰
SEKI. Seme. An ordeal, responsibility.	CHO. Takuwaeru. To store up, lay up.	JI, NI. Futatsu, soeru. Two, to add.	KI. Tattoi, takai. Excellent, valuable, dear, you.	SHA. Morau. To receive.
貶	買	貸	費	貼
HEN. Otosu, herasu. To degrade, reduce.	BAI. Kau. To buy.	TAI. Kasu. To lend.	HI. Tsuieru. To spend, waste, expenses.	CHŌ. Haru. To stick on, a dose of medicine.
貿	賀	賂	賃	賄
BŌ. Akinau. To exchange, trade.	GA. Iwau. To congratulate.	RO. Okuru, mainai. To present, a bribe.	CHIN. Yatou, karu. Hire, rent, wages, fare.	WAI. Mainai, takara. A bribe, wealth.
資	賈	賊	賑	賓
SHI. Tasuke, ukeru, takara. Help, to receive, take, wealth, property.	KO. Akinau, akindo. To trade, a merchant.	ZOKU. Nusubito, sokonau. A robber, rebel, to injure.	SHIN. Nigiwai, nigiwasu. To be bustling, crowded, to help with alms.	HIN. Marōto. A guest.

貝

贊 × SAN. *Homeru, tasukeru.* To praise, assist, second.	**賜** × SHI. *Tamau.* To give (used of a superior).	**賞** × SHŌ. *Yomisuru, tamau, tamamono.* To prize, give to an inferior, reward.	**賠** × BAI. *Ojinau.* To make good, indemnify.	**賢** × KEN. *Kashikoi, sugureru* Clever, to excel.
賣 × BAI. *Uru.* To sell.	**賤** × SEN. *Iyashii.* Low, mean, humble.	**賦** × FU. *Kubaru, mitsugi.* To distribute, taxes.	**質** × SHITSU, SHICHI. *Tadasu, umaretsuki, makoto, sunao.* To enquire, nature, constitution, material, unsophisticated, a pledge.	**賭** × TO. *Kakeru.* To bet, gamble.
賴 × RAI. *Tanomu, yoru, amari.* To rely on, request, the remainder.	**購** × KŌ. *Aganau.* To ransom, atone.	**賽** × SAI. *Kaerimōde.* Visiting a temple, (to present thanks).	**贄** × SHI. *Nie.* Religious offerings, offerings.	**贅** ZEI. *Ibo, sugiru.* A wart, superfluous, excessive.
贈 × SŌ. *Okuru.* To send, present.	**贋** × GAN. *Niseru.* To counterfeit.	**贍** × SEN. *Nigiwasu, sukū.* To furnish supplies, help.	**贏** EI. *Katsu, amari.* To conquer, very, many.	**贔** × HI. *Chikara, okosu.* Strength, to raise.
賊 ZŌ. *Osameru, nusumimono.* To put away, stolen goods.	**贖** SHOKU. *Aganau.* To redeem, atone.			
赤 **赤** × (The 155th Radical) SEKI, SHAKU. *Akai.* Red.	**赦** × SHA. *Yurusu.* To forgive, pardon.	**赧** × TAN. *Akai, haji-gao.* Red, a blush.		

走 ✕	赴 ✕	起 ✕	超 ✕	越 ✕
(The 156th Radical) Sō. Washiru. To run.	Fu. Tsugeru, omomuku, itaru. To announce, go, reach.	Ki. Tatsu, okoru, okosu. To rise, raise, originate.	Chō. Koeru, odori-koeru. To pass over, leap over, surpass.	Etsu. Koeru, kosu. To pass over, cross over.
趣 ✕	趨 ✕			
Shu. Omomuku, omomuki, washiru, sumiyaka. To go, purport, to run, quick.	Sō. Washiru, sumiyaka. To run, quick.			
足 ✕	跋	跛	距 ✕	跡 ✕
(The 157th Radical) Soku. Ashi, taru. A foot, leg, to suffice.	Batsu. Aruku, koeru. To walk, cross over, tread on.	Ha. Ashinae. Lame, a cripple.	Kio. Itaru, fusegu, koeru. To reach, distant from, to defend, cross over.	Seki. Ato. A trace, clew.
跣	跨 ✕	跪	路 ✕	跳
Sen. Hadashi. Barefoot.	Kwa. Matagaru. To straddle, extend across.	Ki. Hizamazuku. To kneel.	Ro. Michi. A road, way.	Chō. Odoru. To leap, dance.
踊 ✕	跣	踏 ✕	踐	踞
Yō. Odoru. To leap, dance.	Sho, so. Tōsu, wakatsu. To pass through, divide, distinguish.	Tō. Fumu. To tread on, trample on.	Sen. Fumu. To tread on, fulfil, ascend.	Kio. Uzukumaru. To squat down, crouch down.
踵 ✕	蹄 ✕	蹂	踰	蹇
Shō. Kibisu, kakato. The heel.	Tei. Hizume. A hoof.	Jū. Fumu. To tread on, trample on.	Yu. Koeru. To cross over.	Ken. Ashinae, izari, nayamu. Lame, a cripple, to be in distress.

走

足

蹙 Shuku. Shikameru, semeru, sumiyaka. To wrinkle, press upon, quick.	蹲 Son. Uzukumaru. To squat down, crouch down.	蹴 Shuku. Keru, fumu. To kick, tread on.	蹤 Shō. Ato. A foot-print, clew, vestige. 踪	躁 Sō. Sawagu. To be excited, tumultuous.
躇 Cho. Tatazumu, tamerau. To stop, hesitate.	躊 Chū. Tatazumu, tamerau. To stop, hesitate.	躍 Yaku. Odoru. To leap, dance.	躓 Chi. Tsumazuku. To stumble.	

身

身 (The 158th Radical) Shin. Mi, mizukara. The body, I, myself, one's self, personal.	躬 Kiū. Mi, mizukara. The body, one's self.	躾 — Shitsuke. Instruction in morals and politeness, cultivation, culture.	軀 Ku. Mi, mukuro. The body, a corpse.	軈 — Yagate. Directly, by and by.

車

車 (The 159th Radical) Sha. Kuruma. A wheel, carriage.	軋 Atsu. Kishiru. To grate.	軌 Ki. Wadachi. A rut, track, line.	軍 Gun. Ikusa, moromoro. War, all.	軒 Ken. Noki. The eaves of a house, numeral for houses.
軟 Nan. Yawaraka. Soft, weak.	軸 Jiku. Yokogami. A stem, stick, axis, axletree.	較 Kaku, Kō. Kuraberu, yaya. To compare, examine, somewhat.	載 Sai. Noseru, toshi. To place on record, a year.	輔 Ho. Tasukeru. To assist, rescue.
輓 Ban. Hiku. To pull.	輕 Kei. Karui, karonzuru. Light, to make light of.	輙 Chō. Tayasui, sunawachi. Easy, that is.	輛 Riō. Kuruma. The numeral used in counting carriages.	輜 Shi. Kuruma. A waggon.

(128)

輝 ✕	輦 ✱	輪 ✕	輩 ✕	輳
Kɪ.	Rᴇɴ.	Rɪɴ.	Hᴀɪ.	Sō.
Hikari, kagayaku.	*Teguruma.*	*Wa, meguru.*	*Tomogara.*	*Atsumaru.*
Light, to shine.	An Imperial carriage.	A ring, wheel, to revolve.	Companions, the editorial "we."	To assemble, collect.
輯 ✕	輸 ✕	輻	輾	輿
Sʜū.	Sʜᴜ, Yᴜ.	Fᴜᴋᴜ.	Tᴇɴ.	Yo.
Atsumeru, osameru.	*Itasu, okuru, makeru.*	*Kuruma no ya, atsumaru.*	*Korogaru, kishiru.*	*Koshi, ninau.*
To control, collect, compile, edit.	To do, send, lose.	The spokes of a wheel, to assemble.	To roll over, grate.	A carriage used by persons of high rank, the world, the public.
轄 ✕	轆轤	轉 ✕	轍	轟 ✕
Kᴀᴛsᴜ.	Rᴏᴋᴜ-ʀᴏ.	Tᴇɴ.	Tᴇᴛsᴜ.	Kwō.
Kusabi.	—	*Meguru, korobi, korogaru, kawaru.*	*Wadachi.*	*Todoroku.*
A wedge, to rule, have jurisdiction over.	A pulley.	To revolve, fall, change.	A rut, precedent.	To rumble.
轢 ✕	轡 ✕			
Rᴇᴋɪ.	Hɪ.			
Kishiru.	*Kutsuwa, kutsuwa-zura.*			
To grate.	A bridle-bit, the reins of a bridle.			
辛 ✕	辟	辨 ✕	辭 ✕	
(The 160th Radical)	Hᴇᴋɪ.	Bᴇɴ.	Jɪ.	
Sʜɪɴ.	*Shirizoku, saru, mesu.*	*Wakimaeru, wakatsu.*	*Kotoba, inamu, itomagoi suru.*	
Karai, karajitte, kanoto.	To retire, depart, call.	To discriminate, discern, control. 辯	Language, to refuse, resign, bid farewell.	
Pungent, bitter, harsh, with much difficulty, barely, the eighth of the ten calendar signs.				
辰 ✕	辱 ✕	農 ✕		
(The 161st Radical)	Jᴏᴋᴜ.	Nō.		
Sʜɪɴ.	*Hyji, katajikenai.*	*Tatsukuri.*		
Tatsu, toki.	Shame, disgrace, thankful, obliged.	Agriculture.		
The dragon, the 5th of the twelve horary characters, time.				

辛

辰

辵
辶 (The 162nd Radical)
CHAKU.
Washiru.
To go, run.

辷	込	迂	迄
—	—	U.	KITSU.
Suberu.	Komi, komu.	Mawaridōi.	Made.
To slip.	Odds given, in gross, a crowd, to put into, crowd into.	Round about.	To, till, as far as, by.

迅	巡	迎	近	返
JIN.	JUN.	GEI.	KIN.	HEN.
Hayai.	Meguru.	Mukaeru.	Chikai.	Kaesu.
Quick.	To go round, patrol, travel about.	To go out to meet, welcome.	Near.	To return.

迚	迪	迫	迭	述
—	TEKI.	HAKU.	TETSU.	JUTSU.
Tote.	Michibiku, susumu, shitagau.	Semaru.	Tagaini, kawaru.	Noberu.
Because, although, by no means (with a negative).	To lead, advance, follow.	To press on, urge.	Mutually, to change.	To state, relate.

迴	迷	迸	迹	追
KWAI.	MEI.	HŌ.	SEKI.	TSUI.
Meguru.	Mayou.	Hotobashiru, shirizokeru.	Ato.	Ou.
To go round, circulate.	To go astray, be bewildered.	To splash, be scattered.	Traces, remains.	To pursue, follow, supplement.

退	送	逃	逆	迯
TAI.	SŌ.	TŌ.	GEKI, GIAKU.	HO.
Shirizoku.	Okuru, hanamuke.	Nigeru.	Sakau sakasama.	Nigeru, nogareru.
To withdraw, retire.	To send, escort, a present to one starting on a journey.	To run away.	To be contrary to, disobey, upside down.	To run away, escape.

逢	透	逐	途	逗
HŌ.	TŌ.	CHIKU.	TO.	TŌ.
Au.	Sukitōru, tōru.	Ou, shitagau.	Michi.	Todomaru.
To meet.	To be transparent, pass through.	To chase, follow, obey.	A road.	To stop.

這 ✕	通 ✕	逝 ✕	逞 ✕	速 ✕
GEN.	TSŪ.	SEI.	TEI.	SOKU.
Kono, mukau.	Tōru, kayou, kayoi.	Yuku, saru.	Takumashii.	Sumiyaka.
This, to face.	To pass through or along, be acquainted with, a street, a pass-book, the numeral for letters, &c.	To go, depart, die.	Powerful.	Quick.

造 ✕	逡	連 †	週 ✕	逮
ZŌ.	SHUN.	REN.	SHŪ.	TAI, TEI.
Tsukuru, itaru.	Shizuru.	Tsuranaru, shikirini.	Meguri, meguru.	Oyobu, ou.
To make, create, build, reach.	To withdraw.	To be arranged in a row, connected, united, continuously.	A revolution, week, to go round.	To reach, chase.

逵	進 †	逸 ✕	遊 ✕	逼
KI.	SHIN.	ITSU.	YŪ.	HIOKU, FUKU.
Tsuji.	Susumu, ageru.	Nogareru, sug:ru, kakureru.	Asobu.	Semaru.
Cross-roads, a thoroughfare. 辻	To advance, be promoted, present.	To escape, exceed, hide.	To play, amuse one's self, travel for pleasure.	To press, urge.

遁 ✕	遂 ✕	遇 ✕	運 ✕	過 ✕
TON.	SUI.	GŪ.	UN.	KWA.
Nigeru, nogareru.	Togeru, tsui ni.	Au, tamatama, aishirau.	Hakobu, meguru.	Sugiru, ayamachi, yogiru, toga.
To run away, escape.	To accomplish, finally.	To meet unexpectedly, occasionally, to entertain.	To transport, revolve, fortune, chance.	To exceed, a mistake, to pass by, a fault.

遏	遐	遑	道 ✕	達
ATSU.	KA.	KWŌ.	DŌ.	TATSU.
Todomeru.	Haruka.	Itoma.	Michi.	Itaru, tōru, todokeru, sonawaru.
To stop.	Far off, indistinct.	Leisure, disengaged.	A road, doctrine, principle.	To reach, pass through, forward, endowed with, adept, to inform, instruct, notify.

違 ✕	遙 ✕	遜	遞 ✕	遠 ✕
I.	YŌ.	SON.	TEI.	EN.
Chigau, tagau.	Haruka.	Herikudaru.	Tsutau, kawaru.	Tōi.
To differ, violate.	Far off, indistinct.	To humble one's self.	To transmit, communicate, change.	Far.

遣 ✗ KEN. *Yaru, tsukawasu.* To give, send, transmit.	遡 So. *Sakanoboru, mukau.* To go against the current, face, to trace up to its source.	適 ✗ TEKI. *Itaru, tamatáma, kanau.* To reach, occasionally, to suit.	遮 ✗ SHA. *Saegiru.* To intercept, block up.
遯 TON. *Nogareru, kakureru.* To escape, hide.	遲 ✗ CHI. *Osoi.* Late, slow.	遶 Jō. *Meguru, matou.* To go round, wrap round.	遵 ✗ JUN. *Shitagau.* To follow, obey.
選 ✗ SEN. *Erabu, hakaru.* To choose, elect, estimate.	遺 ✗ I, YUI. *Okuru, nokosu, wasureru, ushinau.* To leave behind, bequeath, forget, lose.	遼 RIŌ. *Haruka.* Distant.	邀 YŌ. *Motomeru, mukaeru.* To ask for, go to meet.
避 ✗ HI. *Sakeru.* To escape from, avoid.	邁 ✗ HAI, MAI. *Yuku, koeru.* To go, pass over.	邂 KAI. *Tamasaka.* Seldom, unexpectedly, to meet by chance.	還 ✗ KWAN. *Kaeru, kaesu, meguru.* To return, go round.
邈 BAKU. *Haruka.* Far off, indistinct.	邊 ✗ HEN. *Hotori, atari.* Side, place, region.	邏 RA. *Meguru.* To go round, patrol.	
阝 (The 163rd Radical) YŪ. *Ōzato, mura.* A village, city, capital.	邦 ✗ NA, DA. *Nanzo, are, ano.* How, why, that.	邦 ✗ HŌ. *Kuni, sakai.* A country, nation.	邪 ✗ JA. *Yokoshima, ya, ka.* Wicked, heterodox, evil, an interrogative particle.

(133)

郊	郎 ✗	郁 ✗	郡 ✗	部 ✗
Kō.	Rō.	Iku.	Gun.	Bu.
No, katainaka.	Onoko, otoko.	Sakan, kōbashii.	Kōri.	Wakatsu, kumi.
The country, suburbs.	A man, a complimentary term applied to masters, husbands, and sons.	Flourishing, fragrant.	A district, county.	To divide, a section, department, bureau, copy of a book.

郭 ✗	郵 ✗	都 ✗	郷 ✗	鄙 ✗
Kwaku.	Yū.	To.	Kiō, Gō.	Hi.
Kuruwa.	Hitoyado.	Miyako, subete.	Sato, sakini.	Iyashii, hina, inaka.
An enclosure, fortifications.	A post office, mail.	The Capital, all.	A village, previously.	Mean, low, humble, rustic, the country.

鄭	鄰			
Tei.	Rin.			
Nengoro.	Tonari, tonaru.			
Kind, polite, careful, lewd.	Neighbouring, a neighbour, to adjoin.			

酉 ✗	酊 ✗	酋 ✗	酌 ✗	配 ✗	酉
(The 164th Radical) Yū. Tori, umu. The "bird" the 10th of the twelve horary characters, to be satiated.	Tei. You. To be drunk.	Shū. Kashira. The head, chief.	Shaku. Kumu, hakaru. To pour out (as wine), weigh, consider.	Hai. Kubaru. To distribute.	

酎	酒 ✗	酢	酣	酪 ✗
Chū.	Shu.	So.	Kan.	Mei.
Koi sake.	Sake.	Su, sushi.	Takenawa.	You.
Strong liquor, alcohol.	Wine, liquor.	Vinegar, food made of rice and fish, or eggs, with vinegar.	At its height, on the decline.	To be drunk.

酬 ✗	酷 ✗	酸 ✗	醇	醋 ✗
Shū.	Koku.	San.	Jun.	Saku.
Mukuyuru.	Hanahada, itamashii.	Sui.	Moppara, sumizake.	Su.
To repay, give back.	Very, painful, lamentable.	Sour.	Pure, pure wine.	Vinegar, acid.

醉 Sui. *You.* To be drunk.	醒 Sei. *Sameru.* To awake, become sober, fade.	醢 Kai. *Hishio, shishi-bishio.* Pickled mince meat or jelly, salted mince meat.	醜 Shū. *Minikui, ashii.* Ugly, bad.	醬 Shō. *Hishio.* Pickles.
醫 I. *Kusushi, iyasu.* A doctor, to cure.	醸 Kio. *Sakekau.* To buy wine, contribute.	醴 Rei. *Amazake.* Sweet wine.	釀 Jō. *Kamosu.* To brew.	
釆 The 165th Radical) Han, hen. *Wakatsu.* To divide.	釋 Shaku. *Toku, hodoku.* To unfasten, set free, melt, Buddhism.			
里 The 166th Radical) Ri. *Sato.* A Japanese or Chinese mile, village.	重 Chō, Jū. *Omoi, kasanaru, tattobu.* Heavy, important, to be piled up, repeatedly, to honour.	野 Ya. *No, iyashii.* A moor, wild, rustic, low, the country.	量 Riō. *Hakaru, kakeme.* To weigh, estimate, weight, quantity, ability.	釐 Rin, ri. *Osameru.* To regulate, a small copper coin, cash.
金 The 167th Radical) Kin, kon. *Kane, kogane.* Gold, metal, money.	釘 Tei. *Kugi.* A nail.	釜 Fu. *Kama.* A boiler, cauldron.	針 Shin. *Hari.* A needle. 鍼	釣 Chō. *Tsuru.* To fish.
釦 Kō. *Botan.* A button, stud.	釧 Sen. *Tamaki, kanzashi.* A bracelet, hairpin.	釿 Kin. *Chōna.* An adz.	鈍 Ton, don. *Nibui.* Dull, blunt. 鈍	鉛 En. *Namari.* Lead.

鉋	鉢 ✕	鈴 ✕	鉗	鉤
Hō.	Hatsu.	Rei.	Ken, kan.	Kō.
Kanna.	Hachi.	Suzu.	Hodashi.	Kagi, tsuribari.
A carpenter's plane.	A bowl, basin.	A bell.	Shackles, fetters.	A hook.
鉦	銃 ✕	銀 ✕	銅 ✕	銑
Shō.	Jū.	Gin.	Dō.	Sen.
Dora.	Teppō.	Shirogane.	Akagane.	Kigane, zuku.
A gong before a temple.	A gun, firearms.	Silver.	Copper.	Pig iron, unwrought metal.
銚	銘 ✕	鋭 ✕	鋒 ✕	銷
Chō.	Mei.	Ei.	Hō.	Shō.
Sashinabe.	Nazukeru, shirusu, arawasu.	Surudoi, togaru.	Hokosaki, kissaki.	Tokasu, kesu.
A pot with a long spout used for warming sake.	A name, to name, record, publish.	Pointed, sharp, acute.	The point of a spear.	To melt, put out.
鋏 ✕	鋤 ✕	鋪	鋸 ✕	鋼 ✕
Kiō.	Jo.	Ho.	Kio.	Kō.
Kanabasami.	Suku, suki.	Tsuranaru, noberu, shiku, mise.	Nokogiri.	Hagane.
Scissors.	To dig, a spade hoe.	To be arranged in a row, extend, spread, a shop.	A saw.	Steel.
録 ✕	錆	錐	錘	銭 ✕
Roku.	Shō.	Sui.	Tsui.	Sen.
Shirusu.	Sabi.	Kiri.	Hakari no omori.	Zeni.
To write down, records.	Rust.	A gimlet.	A weight, plummet.	Small cash, a cent.
錠 ✕	錦 ✕	錨 ✕	錮	錫 ✕
Jō.	Kin.	Biō.	Ko.	Shaku, seki.
—	Nishiki.	Ikari.	Iru, fusagu.	Suzu, ataeru.
A lock.	Embroidered silk, brocade.	An anchor.	To cast (metal), to shut up.	Tin, to bestow.

(136)

錬	鍋 ✕	鍮	鍛	鍬
REN.	KWA.	CHŪ.	TAN.	SHŌ.
Neru, kitaeru.	*Nabe.*	—	*Kitaeru.*	*Kuwa, suki.*
To temper, forge.	A pot, kettle.	Brass.	To forge, temper.	A hoe, spade.
鍵	鍾	鎗	鎚	鎔
KEN.	SHŌ.	SŌ.	TSUI, TAI.	YŌ.
Kagi.	*Atsumeru, kasaneru, sakazuki.*	*Yari.*	*Kanazuchi.*	*Igata, torakasu.*
A key.	To collect, repeat, a wine-cup.	A spear.	A hammer.	A mould, to melt.
鎖	鎧	鎮 ✕	鏃	鏖 ✕
SA.	GAI.	CHIN.	ZOKU.	Ō.
Kusari, tozasu.	*Yoroi.*	*Shizumeru, yasunjiru, mamoru.*	*Yajiri.*	*Minagoroshi.*
A chain, to shut.	A coat of mail, to wear armour.	To calm, tranquillize, protect, garrison.	The head or barb of an arrow.	Extermination.
鏑	鏝	鏡 ✕	鏤	鏈
TEKI.	MAN.	KIŌ.	RŌ, RU.	REN.
Yajiri, kaburaya.	*Kote.*	*Kagami, akiraka.*	*Chiribameru.*	*Kusari.*
The head or barb of an arrow, an arrow with a turnipshaped head.	A trowel.	A mirror, clear, bright, an example.	To inlay.	A chain.
鐘 ✕	鐙	鐚	鐵 ✕	鐸
SHŌ.	TŌ.	A.	TETSU.	TAKU.
Kane.	*Abumi.*	*Bita.*	*Kurogane.*	*Ōsuzu.*
A bell.	A stirrup.	An iron cash.	Iron. 鉄	A large bell.
鐫	鐮 ✕	鑄 ✕	鑑	鑛 ✕
SEN.	REN.	CHŪ.	KAN.	KWŌ.
Kizamu, eru.	*Kama.*	*Iru.*	*Kagami, kangamiru.*	*Aragane.*
To engrave, carve.	A sickle.	To cast (metal).	A mirror, example, to regard as an example. 鑒	Raw metal.

(137)

鑠	鑢	鑵	鑿	鑰	
Shaku, Reki.	Rio.	Kwan.	Saku.	Yaku.	
Kesu, torakasu, sakan. To put out, melt, flourishing.	Yasuri. A file.	Tsurube. A tin, can, well-bucket.	Nomi, ugatsu, horu. A chisel, to pierce, dig.	Kagi, ebiji. The bolt or catch of a lock, a padlock.	
長 (The 168th Radical) Chō. Nagai, take, tsukasa. Long, old, senior, chief, superior, to grow, increase.	肆 Shi. Ichigura, tsuranaru, tsui ni. A bazaar, storehouse, shop, arranged, finally.				長
門 (The 169th Radical) Mon. Kado. A gate, outside entrance, door, sect.	閃 Sen. Hirameku. To wave, flash.	閉 Hei. Tojiru, fusagu. To shut, stop up.	開 Kai. Hiroku, toku. To open, explain.	閏 Jun. Urū. Intercalary.	門
閑 Kan. Shizuka, itoma. Quiet, leisure.	間 Kan, Ken. Aida, hima. Between, during, leisure, a measure of length, 6 Japanese feet.	閙 Tō. Isogawashii, kamabisushii. Busy, noisy.	閣 Kaku. Takadono. A large building, two storied house, chamber, cabinet.	閨 Kō. Neya. A bedroom. 大| (The Taikō).	
閥 Batsu. Isaoshi, iegara. Merit, good family.	閨 Kei. Neya. A bedroom.	閲 Etsu. Kemisuru. To inspect, review, examine.	閹 En. Henokokiru. An eunuch.	闊 Kwatsu. Hiroi. Broad, wide, liberal.	
閑 Kan. Takenawa. At its height, on the decline.	闇 An. Kurai. Dark.	闃 Geki. Shizuka. Quiet.	闔 Kō. Tobira, tojiru. A door, to shut.	闕 Ketsu. Kakeru, ushinau. The gate of a palace, to lock, lose, confiscate.	

關 Kwan. Kakawaru, tozasu, seki. To concern, shut, a barrier.	闡 Zen. Hiraku, akiraka. To open, clear.	闢 Hiki, hiaku. Hiraku. To open.	
阜 阝 (The 170th Radical) Hiu, Fu. Oka. A mound.	阪 Han. Saka. A road up a hill, an ascent, a hill.	防 Bō. Tsutsumi, fusegu. A dyke, to ward off, defend.	阻 So. Hedateru, kewashii. To be separated from, steep.
陀 Da. Kewashii, sagashii. Steep.	附 Fu. Tsuku, tsukeru. To adhere to, fasten, affix, add.	降 Kō. Kudaru, furu. To come down, descend, rain.	限 Gen. Kagiri, sakai. End, limit, to fix.
陛 Hei. Kizahashi. Steps of the throne. 下 (Heika), Majesty.	陞 Shō. Noboru, susumu. To rise, advance.	陣 Jin. Tsuraneru. A camp, to be arranged in order.	陟 Choku. Noboru, agaru. To rise, advance, be promoted.
除 Jo. Nozoku, hiraku. To subtract, divide, take away.	陪 Bai. Hamberu, tasukeru. To attend on, accompany, assist.	陬 Sō. Sato, sumi. A village, corner.	陰 In. Kage, kakureru, k'moru. Shadow, hidden, cloudy, the female principle in nature, earth.
陳 Chin. Noberu, shiku, hine. To state, spread out, old.	陵 Riō. Misasagi, oka, tsuka. An Imperial tomb, a mound.	陶 Tō. Suemonozukuri. Pottery, a potter.	陷 Kan. Ochiiru, ochiru. To fall into, be entrapped, collapse.

陽 ✕ Yō. *Akiraka, atataka.* Clear, warm, the male principle of nature, Heaven.	隅 ✕ Gu. *Sumi, kado.* A corner, angle.	隆 ✕ Riū. *Takai, sakan.* High, prosperous.	限 ✕ Wai. *Kuma.* Border, edge, shading, a dark spot.	隊 ✕ Tai. *Muragari, ochiru.* A company, regiment, to fall.
隍 ✕ Kwō. *Hori.* A moat.	階 ✕ Kai. *Iizahashi.* Steps, stairs.	隔 ✕ Kaku. *Hedateru.* To be separated from, alternate.	隘 ✕ Ai. *Semai.* Narrow.	隙 ✕ Geki. *Suki, hima.* A crack, opening, leisure.
際 ✕ Sai. *Kiwa, majiwaru.* The edge, time, limit, to associate with.	障 ✕ Shō. *Hedateru, sawari.* To be separated from, an obstacle, hindrance, objection.	隤 ✕ Tai. *Kuzureru, ochiru.* To fall in pieces, go to ruin, fall.	隧 ✕ Sui. *Hikamichi.* An under-ground passage, tunnel.	隨 ✕ Zui. *Shitagau.* To obey, follow, according to.
險 ✕ Ken. *Kewashii.* Steep.	隱 ✕ In, on. *Kakureru.* To hide, be in retirement, secret, illicit, obscure.			
隶 (The 171st Radical) Tai. *Oyobu.* To reach.	隷 Rei. *Tsuku, yakko, shimobe.* To belong to, a servant, menial.			
隹 (The 172nd Radical) Sui. *Furutori.* Birds.	隻 ✕ Seki. *Katagata, hitotsu.* One of a pair, one.	雀 ✕ Jaku. *Suzume.* A sparrow.	雁 ✕ Gan. *Kari.* A wild goose.	雄 ✕ Yū. *Osu.* The male of any animal, strong.

雅 ✗	集	雇	雉 ✗	雌 ✗
Ga.	Shū.	Ko.	Chi.	Shi.
Miyabiyaka.	Atsumeru.	Yatou.	Iji.	Mesu.
Refined, elegant.	To collect, assemble.	To hire, employ.	A pheasant.	The female of any animal, weak.
雍	雖 ✗	雙 ✗	雛 ✗	雜 ✗
Yō.	Sui.	Sō.	Sū.	Zatsu, zō.
Yawaragu, mutsumajii.	Iedomo.	Futatsu. 双	Hina.	Majiwaru, atsumaru.
Tranquil, harmonious.	Although.	Two, a pair, both.	A chicken, small doll.	To m'x, collect, various, miscellaneous, coarse, roughly made.
雞 ✗	離 ✗	難 ✗		
Kei.	Ri.	Nan.		
Niwatori. 鷄	Hanareru, wakatsu.	Katai, nayamu.		
A cock, hen.	To be separated from, divide.	Difficult, hard, to suffer.		
雨 ✗ (The 173rd Radical) U. Ame.	雪 ✗ Setsu. Yuki.	雫 Ta. Shizuku.	雲 ✗ Un. Kumo.	電 ✗ Den. Inazuma, inabikari.
Rain.	Snow, to wash, purify.	A drop.	A cloud.	Lightning, electricity, to telegraph.
雹 Haku. Arare.	零 ✗ Rei. Ochiru.	雷 ✗ Rai. Ikazuchi, kaminari.	需 ✗ Ju. Motomeru.	霄 ✗ Shō. Sora.
Hail.	To fall, a cipher, nought.	Thunder.	To ask for, demand.	The sky, heaven.
震 ✗ Shin. Furū.	霑 Ten. Uruosu, hitasu.	霓 Gei. Niji.	霖 Rin. Nagaame.	霙 Ei. Mizore.
To shake, quake.	To moisten, soak, bestow favours.	A rainbow.	A long continued rain.	Sleet.

霜 ✕	霞 ✕	霤	霧 ✕	霰
Sŏ.	Ka.	Riū.	Mu.	Sen.
Shimo.	*Kasumu.*	*Amadari, shita-tari.*	*Kiri.*	*Arare, mizore.*
Hoar-frost.	To be hazy, mist, haze.	Rain dropping from the eaves.	Mist.	Hail, sleet.
露 ✕	霹	霽	靄	靈 ✕
Ro.	Heki.	Sei.	Ai.	Rei.
Tsuyu, arawareru.	*Hatatagami.*	*Hareru.*	*Kasumu.*	*Tamashii, mitama*
Dew, to be known, manifest.	Thunder or lightning.	To clear up.	To be hazy.	The soul, spirit, ghost, sacred.
靉				
Ai.				
Tanabiku.				
To be spread out, like clouds or smoke.				
青 ✕ (The 174th Radical) Sei. *Aoi.* Green, blue, unripe, inexperienced.	靖 ✕ Sei. *Yasui, osameru.* Quiet, to tranquillize, pacify.	靜 ✕ Sei. *Shizuka.* Quiet, peaceful.		
非 (The 175th Radical) Hi. *Arazu, ashii, soshiru.* Not, bad, wrong, to slander, criticize, blame.	靡 Hi. *Nabiku, nai.* To bend, yield to, wave, obey, not.			
面 (The 176th Radical) Men. *Omote, kao.* The face, front, surface.	靨 Yō. *Ekubo.* A dimple in the cheek.			

青

非

面

革	革 × (The 177th Radical) KAKU. *Kawa, aratameru.* A skin, hide, leather, to renew, restore.	靴 × KWA. *Kutsu.* Boots, shoes.	鞄 HAKU, HŌ. *Kaban.* A bag, portmanteau.	鞋 AI. *Waraji, kawa-gutsu.* A straw sandal, leather-boots.	鞍 × AN. *Kura.* A saddle.
	鞏 KIŌ. *Katai, katameru.* Hard, firm, to harden.	鞘 SHŌ. *Katana no saya.* A sheath, scabbard.	鞠 KIKU. *Mari, osu, yashinau, kiwameru, tsugeru.* A ball, to push, nourish, investigate thoroughly, announce.	鞭 × BEN. *Muchi.* A whip.	韃 BETSU. *Uwagutsu, tabi.* Slippers, stockings, hose.
韋	(The 178th Radical) I. *Oshikawa, somuku.* Tanned and soft leather, to oppose.	韓 × KAN. *Igaki.* A fence, Corea.			
韭	韭 (The 179th Radical) KIŌ. *Nira.* A leek.				
音	音 × (The 180th Radical) IN, ON. *Koe, oto, ne.* Voice, sound, tone, noise.	韻 × IN. *Hibiki.* A rhyming syllable, rhyme, harmonious sound.	響 × KIŌ. *Hibiki, hibiku.* Sound, noise, report, echo, shock.		
頁	頁 × (The 181st Radical) KETSU. *Kashira, kōbe.* The head.	頂 × CHŌ. *Itadaki, itadaku.* The top, head, to put on the head, receive.	頃 × KEI, KIŌ. *Shibaraku, koro.* For some time, a moment.	項 × KŌ. *Unaji.* The nape of the neck.	頌 × SHŌ. *Homeru, utau.* To praise, sing.

(143)

順	須	頑	預	頒
Jun.	Su, shu.	Gwan.	Yo.	Han.
Shitagau, tsuizuru, yawaraka.	Subekaraku, motomeru, mutsu.	Katakuna.	Azukaru, arakajime.	Wakatsu, shiragamajiri.
Order, to obey, follow in regular order, gentle.	Ought, proper, to ask for, wait, an instant.	Obstinate, bigoted.	To have charge of, be entrusted with, previous, preliminary.	To divide, publish abroad, grizzled.
頓	頗	領	頤	頽
Ton.	Ha.	Rei, riō.	I.	Tai.
Yagate, niwaka ni, kashira sageru.	Kata oru, sukoburu.	Kubi, eri, suberu, osameru.	Otogai.	Kuzureru.
Forthwith, suddenly, to bow the head, salute.	To incline to one side, very.	The neck, collar, to rule, govern, jurisdiction, dominion, territory.	The chin.	To fall to pieces, crumble away, fall into decay.
頭	頬	頷	頸	頻
Tō.	Kiō.	Gan.	Kei, kiō.	Hin.
Kashira, kōbe, hotori.	Hō.	Otogai, unazuku.	Kubi.	Shikiri ni.
The head, top, chief, neighbourhood, a classifier of cattle, &c.	The cheek.	The chin, to nod in assent.	The neck, throat, an isthmus.	Constantly.
題	額	顔	願	顛
Dai.	Gaku.	Gan.	Gwan.	Ten.
Arawasu, nazukeru.	Taka, hitai.	Kao.	Negau.	Itadaki, sakasama.
A subject, topic, text, to disclose, name.	The amount, tablet, forehead, a picture, doorplate, price.	The face.	To ask, request, desire, be a candidate for.	The top, head, beginning, upside down.
類	顧	顕	顰	
Rui.	Ko.	Ken, ghn.	Hin.	
Tagui, nitaru.	Kaerimiru, omou, kaette.	Arawareru, akiraka.	Hisomeru.	
Sort, kind, to resemble.	To look back on, reflect, consider, on the contrary.	To be revealed, appear, clear.	To wrinkle, contract, frown.	
風	飄			
(The 182nd Radical) Fū.	Hiō.			
Kaze, narawashi.	Hirugaeru.			
Wind, air, fashion, customs.	To be blown about by the wind, wave.			

(144)

飛				
(The 183rd Radical) HI. *Tobu.* To fly.	翻 HAN, HON. *Hirugaeru.* To turn over, be blown about by the wind, wave, change about, translate.			

食				
(The 184th Radical) SHOKU, JIKI. *Meshi, kū.* Boiled rice, to eat.	飢 KI. *Ueru.* To be hungry, starved, famished.	飫 YO. *Aku, itou.* To be satisfied, tired.	飲 IN. *Nomu, nomimono.* To drink, drink, to suck in the breath.	飯 HAN. *Ii, meshi.* Boiled rice, food.
飽 HŌ. *Aku.* To have enough, be tired of.	飴 I. *Ame.* A kind of jelly made of flour.	飼 SHI. *Kau, yashinau.* To keep, nourish.	飾 SHOKU. *Kazaru.* An ornament, embellishment, to adorn, gloss over.	餅 HEI. *Mochi.* Rice-bread, a cake of rice.
養 YŌ. *Yashinau, sodateru.* To nourish, support, rear, train, cultivate.	餉 SHŌ. *Kareii.* Boiled rice dried, provisions (for troops).	餌 JI. *Eba.* The food of animals, birds, or fishes, bait.	餃 TAI. *Ueru, azareru.* To be starved, famished, tainted.	餓 GA. *Ueru.* To be starved, famished.
餘 YO. *Amari, nokori.* The remainder, surplus, to be left over, too, more than, besides.	餞 SEN. *Hanamuke.* A present given to one setting out on a journey, or to a bride.	餡 AN. *An.* A mixture of beans and sugar used for baking cakes.	館 KWAN. *Yakata, tachi.* A palace, mansion, public office, lodging place.	饅 MAN. — A wheaten cake, dumpling. 頭 (Man jū).
饉 KIN. *Ueru.* To be starved, famished.	饑 KI. *Ueru.* To be starved, famished.	饒 JŌ, NIŌ. *Amaru, yutaka.* Surplus, abundant, liberal, fertile.	饐 I. *Sueru.* To be spoiled, stale.	饗 KIŌ. *Motenasu, sakamori.* To entertain guests, a banquet.

饜 EN. *Aku.* To have eaten to satiety, be satisfied.				
首 (The 185th Radical) SHU, SHŪ. *Kōbe, kashira.* The head, chief, to acknowledge, confess.				
香 (The 186th Radical) KŌ. *Nioi.* Odour, fragrance, incense.	馨 KEI, KIŌ. *Kōbashii, kaoru.* Fragrant, incense.			
馬 (The 187th Radical) BA, ME. *Uma.* A horse.	馭 GIO. *Noru, osameru.* To ride, drive, rule.	駄 TA, DA. *Owaseru.* The numeral for horse-loads, to put a load on (a horse).	馳 CHI. *Haseru.* To ride fast, gallop, urge on.	馴 JUN. *Nareru, shitagau.* To be accustomed to, familiar with, follow, obey.
駁 HAKU. *Buchi-uma.* A piebald horse.	駟 SHI. *Yotsu no uma.* Four horses.	駐 CHŪ. *Todomaru.* To stop, reside.	駑 DO. *Oso-uma.* A slow horse, stupid.	駒 KU. *Koma.* A colt.
駕 GA. *Noru, uma wo kuruma ni tsukeru, shinogu.* To ride, harness a horse to a waggon, endure.	駛 SHI. *Toi, hayai.* Quick.	駭 GAI. *Odoroku.* To be frightened.	駱 RAKU. *Kawarake-uma.* A horse with black mane, a camel. 駝 (*Raku-da*).	騁 HEI. *Haseru, washiru.* To gallop, hasten, urge on.

駿 * Shun. *Sugureta uma, toi.* An excellent horse, quick.	騎 * Ki. *Noru, matagaru.* To ride, sit astride of, the numeral for horsemen.	騙 * Hen. *Sukasu, damasu.* To cheat, deceive.	騰 * Tō. *Noboru, agaru, kinkiriuma.* To rise, ascend, a gelding.	騷. Sō. *Sawagu.* To be noisy, tumultuous, excited.
驃 * Hiō. *Isamu, haseru.* To be bold, courageous, to hasten, urge on.	驅 * Ku. *Kakeru, karu, washiru.* To run, hurry, urge on.	驍 * Kiō. *Sugureta uma, takei.* An excellent horse, strong, fierce.	驕 * Kiō. *No-uma, ogoru.* A wild horse, stubborn, proud.	驚 * Kei, kiō. *Odoroku.* To be frightened.
驗 * Ken. *Shirushi, kangaeru.* A mark, proof, to consider, examine.	驛 * Eki. *Umayado, umaya.* A post station, station.	驢 Ro. *Usagi-uma.* A donkey.		
骨 (The 188th Radical) Kotsu. *Hone.* A bone.	骸 Gai. *Hone.* A bone, the bones of the body.	體 * Tei, tai. *Karada, katachi.* Body, person, substance, appearance.	髑 Doku. *Hitogashira, sarekōbe.* The skull. 髑 (*Doku-ro*).	
高 * (The 189th Radical) Kō. *Takai.* High, lofty, dear, good, august.				
髟 * (The 190th Radical) Hiō. *Nagai kami no ke.* Long hair.	髢 Tei. *Kazura, kamoji.* A wig, false hair.	髭 Shi. *Uwahige.* Moustache.	髮 * Hatsu. *Kami.* Hair (human).	髷 Kioku. *Mage.* The Japanese cue, the hair dressed in the manner of Japanese women.

骨

高

髟

髻 KITSU, KETSU. *Motodori, mage.* The Japanese cue, the hair dressed in the manner of Japanese women.	髮 BIN. — The hair on the temples, whiskers.	鬣 RIŌ. *Tategami.* A horse's mane.	鬘 MAN. *Kazura.* A wig.	
鬥 (The 191st Radical) TŌ. *Tatakau.* To fight.	鬩 GEKI. *Semegu, tatakau.* To quarrel, blame.	鬪 TŌ. *Tatakau, arasou.* To fight, contend for.	鬮 KIŪ. *Kuji, kujitoru.* A lot, to draw lots.	
鬯 (The 192nd Radical) CHŌ. *Kaorigusa.* Fragrant herbs.	鬱 UTSU. *Fusagaru, shigeru.* Gloomy, dull, melancholy, dense.			
鬲 (The 193rd Radical) REKI, KAKU. *Ashiganae.* A tripod.	鬻 IKU. *Hisagu.* To hawk goods, peddle, sell.			
鬼 (The 194th Radical) KI. *Oni.* A devil, ghost, spirit.	魁 KWAI. *Kashira, sakigake, ii naru.* Head, leader, large, great.	魂 KON. *Tamashii.* The soul, spirit, ghost.	魄 HAKU. *Tamashii.* The soul, spirit, ghost.	魅 BI, MI. *Sudama, bakasu.* A hobgoblin, to delude, bewitch.
魃 HATSU. *Hideri no kami.* The demon of drought, drought.	魔 MA. *Oni.* An evil spirit, devil.	魘 EN. *Osowareru.* Attacked by evil spirits, to have the nightmare.		

(148)

魚					
魚 (The 195th Radical) GIO. *Uwo, toto.* A fish.	漁 GIO. *Sunadoru.* To fish, a fisherman.	魯 RO. *Oroka, nibui.* Foolish, dull.	鮑 HŌ. *Awabi.* The sea-ear, (*haliotis*).	鮎 TEN. *Ayu.* A river fish resembling a trout.
鮒 FU. *Funa.* A fresh water fish like a carp.	鮭 KEI. *Shake, sake.* A salmon.	鮫 KŌ. *Same.* A shark.	鮪 I. *Shibi.* A tunny, bonito.	鮮 SEN. *Nama-uwo, akiraka, azayaka, sukunai.* Fresh fish, clear, bright, fresh, few.
鯉 RI. *Koi.* A carp.	鯰 NEN. *Namazu.* The cat fish.	鯖 SEI. *Saba.* Mackerel.	鯛 CHŌ. *Tai.* The *tai*, the favourite fish of the Japanese, resembling a perch.	鯡 HI. *Nishin.* Herring.
鯣 EKI. *Surume, akai suzuki.* Dried cuttle fish, red perch.	鯨 KEI. *Kujira.* A whale.	鰈 TŌ. *Karei.* A sole.	鰒 FUKU. *Awabi.* The sea-ear, (*haliotis*).	鰓 SAI. *Agito, era.* The gills of a fish.
鰕 KA. *Ebi.* A shrimp, prawn.	鯔 RIŪ. *Bora.* The mullet.	鰯 — *Iwashi.* A sardine.	鰥 KWAN. *Yamo-o.* A widower.	鰭 KI. *Hire.* The fins of a fish.
鰹 KEN. *Katsuo.* The bonito.	鰻 MAN. *Unagi.* An eel.	鰾 HIŌ. *Nibe.* A fish's air bladder, isinglass, glue.	鱆 SHŌ. *Tako.* An octopus.	鱈 SETSU. *Tara.* The cod.

(149)

鱒	鱗 ✕	鱧	鱷	鱸
Son.	Rin.	Rei.	Gaku.	Ro.
Masu.	*Uroko, koke.*	*Hamo.*	*Wani.*	*Suzuki.*
Salmon-trout.	The scales of a fish or snake.	A kind of eel.	An alligator, crocodile. 鰐	A perch.
鳥 ✕ (The 196th Radical) Chō. *Tori.* A bird.	鳩 ✕ Kiū. *Hato.* A pigeon.	鳳 ✕ Hō. — The phoenix, a fabulous and felicitous bird. 凰 (*Hō-ō*).	鳶 En. *Tobi.* A fish-hawk, kite.	鴆 Chin. *Ashimonodori.* The secretary bird, a poisonous bird, poisonous.	鳥
鴈 Gan. *Kari.* A wild goose.	鴉 A. *Karasu.* A crow.	鴒 Rei. *Ishidataki.* The water wag-tail. 鶺	(*Seki-rei*).	鴕 Da. — The ostrich.	鳥 (*Da-chō*).	鴛 En. *Oshidori.* The drake of the mandarin duck. 鴦 (*En-ō*, Mandarin ducks).
鴨 ✕ Ō. *Kamo.* A wild duck, mallard.	鴻 ✕ Kō. *Ō-gari, ōi naru.* A large wild goose, large, great.	鴟 Shi. *Tobi.* A hawk, kite. 鷗	鵝 Ga. *Ahiru.* A tame goose.	鵠 Koku. *Kugui.* The swan.
鵜 Tei. *U.* The cormorant.	鵯 Hitsu. *Hiyodori.* The brown-eared bulbul.	鵬 Bō. — A huge fabulous bird.	鵲 Jaku. *Kasasagi.* The magpie.	鶉 Jun. *Uzura.* A quail.
鶩 Bu, boku. *Ahiru.* A tame duck.	鶯 ✕ Ō. *Uguisu.* The Japanese nightingale (Cettria cantans).	鶴 ✕ Kaku, kwaku. *Tsuru, shiroi.* The stork, white.	鷗 O. *Kamome.* A sea-gull.	鷲 ✕ Shū. *Washi.* An eagle.

	鷸 ITSU. Shigi. A snipe.	鷹 YŌ. Taka. A hawk, falcon.	鷺 RO. Sagi, shirasagi. The snowy heron, egret.	鸚 Ō. Monoii-dori. The parrot. 丨鵡 (Ō-mu).	鸞 RAN. — The phoenix.
鹵	鹵 (The 197th Radical) RO. Shiohama. A salt beach, salt.	鹹 KAN. Shiohayui. Salty, brackish.	鹼 KEN. Shiohayui. Salty, carbonate of soda used for soap. 石丨 (Sek-ken, Soap).	鹽 EN. Shio. Salt.	
鹿	鹿 (The 198th Radical) ROKU. Shika, ka. A deer, stag.	麓 ROKU. Fumoto. The foot of a mountain.	麗 REI. Uruwashii, yoi, akiraka. Beautiful, good, bright.	麝 JA. Kaori-jika. Musk deer. 丨香 (Ja-kō).	麟 RIN. — The unicorn. 麒丨 (Ki-rin).
	麤 SO. Arai, oroka. Rough, coarse, foolish.				
麥	麥 (The 199th Radical) BAKU. Mugi. Wheat.	麩 FU. Mugikasu. A kind of food made of wheat flour, wheat bran.	麹 KIKU. Kōji. Barm, yeast.	麵 MEN. Mugi no ko. Wheat flour. 丨包 (Mem-pō, Bread).	
麻	麻 (The 200th Radical) MA. Asa. Hemp.	麾 KI. Hata, sashimaneku. A signal flag, to beckon.			

黄 (The 201st Radical) Kwō, ō. Ki. Yellow.					
黍 (The 202nd Radical) Sho. Kibi. Millet.	黐 Ri. Torimochi, nebaru. Bird lime, sticky.				
黒 (The 203rd Radical) Koku. Kuroi. Black.	默 Boku, moku. Damaru, modasu. To be silent.	黛 Tai. Mayuzumi. The paint used to blacken the eyebrows, black.	黜 Chutsu. Shirizokeru. To send away, drive away, degrade.	點 Ten. Shirusu, osu. A dot, mark, point, spot, to mark, light, nod, punctuate.
鯨 Gei. Irezumi. Brands marked on a criminal.	黨 Tō. Mure, tomogara, tagui. A band, association, party, companions, sort.	黯 An. Kurai. Dark, gloomy.	黴 Bi, mi, bai. Kabi. Mould, mildew.		
黹 (The 204th Radical) Chi. Nuimono. Embroidery.					
黽 (The 205th Radical) Bin, bō. Kaeru. A frog, toad.	鼈 Betsu. Suppon, umigame. A turtle, tortoise.				

鼎	鼎 ✕ (The 206th Radical) TEI, CHŌ. *Kanae.* A tripod, cauldron with three legs and two ears.				
鼓	鼓 ✕ (The 207th Radical) KO, KU. *Tsuzumi.* A drum.				
鼠	鼠 ✕ (The 208th Radical) SO, SHO. *Nezumi.* A rat.	鼬 YŪ. *Itachi.* A weasel.			
鼻	鼻 ✕ (The 209th Radical) BI. *Hana.* The nose.	鼾 KAN. *Ibiki.* Snoring.			
齊	齊 ✕ (The 210th Radical) SEI. *Hitoshii, totonou.* Alike, even, to regulate.	齋 ✕ SAI. *Monoimu, toki, isagiyoi.* Fasting and purification, pure, the meals of Buddhists, a room, study.	齎 ✕ SHI, SEI. *Motarasu, sonaeru.* To cause to carry, present.		
齒	齒 ✕ (The 211st Radical) SHI. *Ha, yowai.* Teeth, age.	齟 SO. *Kuichigu, kamu.* To cross each other, disagree, bite, uneven.	齡 REI. *Yowai, toshi.* Age.	齦 GIN, KON. *Haguki, kamu.* The gums, to bite, chew.	齬 GO. *Kuichigu.* To cross each other, disagree, uneven.

齷 AKU. *Ha aichigai.* Crowded. ❘ 齪 (*Aku-soku*).					
龍 ∕ (The 212nd Radical) RIŪ, RIŪ. *Tatsu.* A dragon, Imperial.					
龜 ∕ (The 213rd Radical) KI. *Kame.* A tortoise.					
龠 ∕ (The 214th Radical) YAKU. *Fue.* A flute.					

APPENDIX.

NANORI. 名乘

Akiie.	顕	家	Hirobumi.	博	文
Akiomi.	章	臣	Hiromasa.	寛	當
Akitake.	章	毅	Hiroyasu.	廣	裕
Akiyoshi.	晃	芳	Hiroyuki.	弘	幸
Akiyuki.	章	之	Hisamoto.	久	元
Aritomo.	有	朋	Hisanori.	壽	昇
Atsumori.	敦	盛	Hisatsugu.	久	継
Fumioki.	文	與	Isao.	勳	
Fusachika.	房	親	Iwao.	巖	
Harumi.	治	躬	Kanenari.	兼	済
Harunobu.	晴	信	Kanesada.	包	定
Hideharu.	秀	陽	Kanetaka.	同	孝
Hidenobu.	頴	信	Katakiyo.	賢	精
Hidetaka.	榮	孝	Katazane.	方	實
Hidetoshi.	秀	俊	Katsumi.	克	巳
Hidetoshi.	英	敏	Kazumasu.	一	盆
Hideyoshi.	秀	吉	Kazunori.	和	志
Hidezumi.	榮	澄	Kazuuji.	和	氏
Hiroaki.	寛	彰	Kimiharu.	公	張

Kiyohiko.	潔	彥	Masayasu.	昌	綏
Kiyokata.	清	堅	Masayoshi.	雅	美
Kiyotaka.	清	隆	Masayuki.	昌	幸
Korenao.	維	直	Masunori.	益	謙
Korenori.	以	矩	Michikuni.	道	邦
Koretaka.	惟	孝	Michinori.	通	軌
Koreyasu.	維	寧	Michitomo.	通	倫
Kototaka.	功	隆	Michiyoshi.	通	祐
Kunikiyo.	邦	愷	Migaku.	琢	
Kimimochi.	公	望	Mimori.	身	守
Masachika.	應	親	Mitsuhide.	光	華
Masahira.	正	衡	Mitsuho.	滿	穗
Masakado.	將	門	Mitsunobu.	盈	信
Masakage.	昌	景	Mitsutsugu.	光	承
Masanaga.	誠	修	Morikata.	守	固
Masanori.	尙	矩	Moritsugu.	衞	次
Masanori.	正	儀	Moronao.	師	直
Masashige.	正	成	Moroyuki.	師	行
Masataka.	尙	貴	Motochika.	元	親
Masatomo.	尙	友	Motonari.	元	就
Masatsura.	正	行	Motouji.	基	氏
Masayasu.	正	懿	Motoyuki.	幹	之

Munemitsu.	宗	光	Sajimitsu.	福	光	
Munenobu.	宗	陳	Sanehira.	實	平	
Munenori.	宗	德	Sanetomi.	實	美	
Munetō.	致	遠	Shigeatsu.	重	叺	
Nagayoshi.	長	慶	Shigefusa.	重	總	
Naosuke.	直	弼	Shigeki.	繁	樹	
Narisue.	成	季	Shigenori.	重	禮	
Naritaka.	齊	高	Shigetoshi.	重	威	
Nobuaki.	伸	顯	Shigezumi.	重	鎭	
Nobunori.	信	規	Shizue.	靜	枝	
Nobusuke.	宜	祐	Shizunaga.	靜	脩	
Nobutake.	信	剛	Sukechika.	祐	親	
Nobuyo.	延	世	Sukenori.	祐	準	
Norimura.	則	村	Sumiyoshi.	純	義	
Norisuke.	範	資	Tadachika.	忠	隣	
Noritsugu.	範	叙	Tadafuyu.	直	冬	
Noritsuna.	職	綱	Tadakazu.	直	員	
Noritsune.	敎	經	Tadanori.	忠	誨	
Noriyori.	範	賴	Tadasu.	蓋		
Norizumi.	諫	澄	Tadatsune.	忠	常	
Sadaaki.	貞	曉	Tadayoshi.	直	義	
Sajihisa.	祥	久	Tadayuki.	直	遁	

Takanori.	喬	則	Toshikata.	紀	賢
Takauji.	尊	氏	Toshinori.	載	憲
Takeaki.	武	揚	Toshisuke.	俊	亮
Takeakira.	健	明	Toshiyuki.	敏	行
Takeo.	猛	雄	Toyokazu.	豐	材
Taketoshi.	武	敏	Toyomi.	豐	躬
Tametomo.	爲	朝	Tsuminaga.	積	壽
Tanetora.	胤	寅	Tsunemoto.	經	本
Tatsuakira.	龍	章	Tsunetane.	常	胤
Terumura.	暉	邑	Tsuneyuki.	庸	行
Terutora.	輝	虎	Tsurasuke.	連	亮
Tokihiro.	辰	熙	Yasuhiro.	恭	寬
Tokimasa.	時	政	Yasumasa.	保	匡
Tokimune.	時	致	Yasunobu.	順	暢
Tokiyoshi.	時	能	Yasunori.	恭	矩
Tomochika.	知	幾	Yasushi.	靖	
Tomomi.	具	視	Yasutoki.	恭	時
Tomomitsu.	知	周	Yasutoshi.	惠	敏
Tomomori.	知	盛	Yasuyuki.	康	行
Tōru.	享		Yasuya.	康	哉
Tōru.	徹		Yorifusa.	頼	房
Toshiie.	利	家	Yorihisa.	頼	佁

Yorimasa.	頼	政	Yoshinori.	佳	積	
Yorimichi.	從	道	Yoshinori.	義	度	
Yoriyuki.	頼	之	Yoshioki.	義	興	
Yoriyuki.	由	之	Yoshisada.	義	貞	
Yoshiaki.	義	昭	Yoshisato.	義	郷	
Yoshiatsu.	敬	温	Yoshitada.	義	賀	
Yoshihisa.	佳	久	Yoshitaka.	可	高	
Yoshika.	良	馨	Yoshiyasu.	好	順	
Yoshimasa.	賀	昌	Yoshitō.	良	任	
Yoshimitsu.	義	滿	Yoshitomo.	義	朝	
Yoshimoto.	良	翰	Yoshitsugu.	義	嗣	
Yoshimoto.	良	基	Yukimichi.	志	道	
Yoshinari.	好	生	Yukitaka.	幸	隆	
Yoshinari.	良	業	Yukitsuna.	雪	綱	
Yoshinobu.	慶	喜	Yukizane.	行	眞	
Yoshinori.	能	憲				

PROVINCES OF JAPAN.　國　名

Gokinai.	五	畿	内	Izumi.	和	泉
Yamashiro.	山		城	Settsu.	攝	津
Yamato.	大		和	Tōkaidō.	東 海	道
Kawachi.	河		内	Iga.	伊	賀

Ise.	伊	勢	Iwashiro.	岩	代
Shima.	志	摩	Rikuzen.	陸	前
Owari.	尾	張	Rikuchū.	陸	中
Mikawa.	三	河	Mutsu (Michinoku).	陸	奥
Tōtōmi.	遠	江	Uzen	羽	前
Suruga.	駿	河	Ugo.	羽	後
Kai.	甲	斐	Hokurikudō.	北 陸	道
Izu.	伊	豆	Wakasa.	若	狹
Sagami.	相	摸	Echizen.	越	前
Musashi.	武	藏	Kaga.	加	賀
Awa.	安	房	Noto.	能	登
Kazusa.	上	總	Etchū.	越	中
Shimōsa.	下	總	Echigo.	越	後
Hitachi.	常	陸	Sado.	佐	渡
Tōsandō.	東 山	道	Sanindō.	山 陰	道
Ōmi.	近	江	Tamba.	丹	波
Mino.	美	濃	Tango.	丹	後
Hida.	飛	彈	Tajima.	但	馬
Shinano.	信	濃	Inaba.	因	幡
Kōzuke.	上	野	Hōki.	伯	耆
Shimotsuke.	下	野	Izumo.	出	雲
Iwaki.	磐	城	Iwami.	石	見

Oki.		隱 岐	Bungo.		豊 後
SANYŌDŌ.		山 陽 道	Hizen.		肥 前
Harima.		播 磨	Higo.		肥 後
Mimasaka.		美 作	Hiuga.		日 向
Bizen.		備 前	Ōsumi.		大 隅
Bitchū.		備 中	Satsuma.		薩 摩
Bingo.		備 後	Iki.		壹 岐
Aki.		安 藝	Tsushima.		對 馬
Suwo.		周 防	Gotō (Island).		五 島
Nagato.		長 門	HOKKAIDŌ.		北 海 道
NANKAIDŌ.		南 海 道	Oshima.		渡 島
Kii.		紀 伊	Shiribeshi.		後 志
Awaji.		淡 路	Ishikari.		石 狩
Awa.		阿 波	Teshio.		天 鹽
Sanuki.		讃 岐	Kitami.		北 見
Iyo.		伊 豫	Iburi.		膽 振
Tosa.		土 佐	Hidaka.		日 高
SAIKAIDŌ.		西 海 道	Tokachi.		十 勝
Chikuzen.		筑 前	Kushiro.		釧 路
Chikugo.		筑 後	Nemuro.		根 室
Buzen.		豊 前	Chishima.		千 島

FU AND KEN.　　　　府　縣

Tōkiō Fu.	東京府	Miyagi Ken.	宮城縣
Kiōto ,,	京都府	Fukushima ,,	福島縣
Ōsaka ,,	大阪府	Iwate ,,	岩手縣
Hokkaidōchō.	北海道廳	Aomori ,,	青森縣
Kanagawa Ken.	神奈川縣	Yamagata ,,	山形縣
Hiōgo ,,	兵庫縣	Akita ,,	秋田縣
Nagasaki. ,,	長崎縣	Fukui ,,	福井縣
Niigata Ken.	新潟縣	Ishikawa ,,	石川縣
Saitama Ken.	埼玉縣	Toyama ,,	富山縣
Gumma ,,	群馬縣	Tottori ,,	鳥取縣
Chiba ,,	千葉縣	Shimane ,,	島根縣
Ibaraki ,,	茨木縣	Okayama ,,	岡山縣
Tochigi ,,	栃木縣	Hiroshima ,,	廣島縣
Nara ,,	奈良縣	Yamaguchi ,,	山口縣
Miye ,,	三重縣	Wakayama ,,	和歌山縣
Aichi ,,	愛知縣	Tokushima ,,	德島縣
Shizuoka ,,	靜岡縣	Kagawa ,,	香川縣
Yamanashi ,,	山梨縣	Ehime ,,	愛媛縣
Shiga ,,	滋賀縣	Kōchi ,,	高知縣
Gifu ,,	岐阜縣	Fukuoka ,,	福岡縣
Nagano ,,	長野縣	Oita ,,	大分縣

Saga Ken.	佐 賀 縣	Kagoshima Ken.	鹿兒島縣
Kumamoto ,,	熊 本 縣	Okinawa ,,	沖 繩 縣
Miyazaki ,,	宮 崎 縣		

GOVERNMENT OFFICES.　官　衙

Cabinet, (Naikaku).	內　閣	Admiralty Department, (Kai-gun-shō).	海 軍 省
Privy Council, (Sūmitsu-In).	樞 密 院	Department of Justice, (Shi-hō-shō).	司 法 省
Imperial Household Department, (Kunaishō).	宮 內 省	Department of Education, (Mom-bu-shō).	文 部 省
Foreign Department, (Gwai-mu-shō).	外 務 省	Department of Agriculture and Commerce, (Nō-shō-mu-shō).	農商務省
Home Department, (Nai-mu-shō).	內 務 省	Department of Communications, (Tei-shin-shō).	遞 信 省
Finance Department, (Ō-kura-shō).	大 藏 省	Upper House (in the Diet), Kizoku-In).	貴 族 院
War Department, (Riku-gun-shō).	陸 軍 省	Lower House (in the Diet), (Shūgi-In).	衆 議 院

NAMES OF COUNTRIES, ETC.　國　名

Aden.	亞　丁	Arctic Ocean, (Hokuyō).	北　洋
Africa.	亞非利加	Asia.	亞 細 亞
Amoy.	廈　門	Atlantic Ocean, (Taiseiyō).	大 西 洋
Annam.	安　南	Australia.	濠　州
Anping.	安　平	Austria.	澳 地 利
Antarctic Ocean,(Nanyō).	南　洋	Bangkok.	盤　谷
Arabia.	亞剌比亞	Belgium.	白 耳 義

Berlin.	伯林	Fusan.	釜山
Black Sea, (Kokkai).	黑海	Germany.	獨逸
Bombay.	孟買	Greece.	希臘
Brazil.	伯拉耳爾	Gulf of Pechili, (Bok-kai).	渤海
Brussels.	巴西	Hawaii.	布哇
Burmah.	緬甸	Holland.	和蘭
Canada.	加奈陀	Hongkong.	香港
Canton.	廣東	India, (Tenjiku).	印度,天竺
Ceylon.	錫闌	Inland Sea, (Seto-uchi).	瀨戶內
Chefoo.	芝罘	Italy.	伊太利
Chemulpo, (Nin-sen).	仁川	London.	倫敦
Chile.	智利	Loochoo Is, (Riūkiū).	琉球
China.	支那,清國	Macao.	澳門
Chungking.	重慶	Madagascar.	馬達加斯加爾
Constantinople.	君士坦丁堡	Malay Peninsula.	巫來半島
Corea, (Chō-sen).	朝鮮	Manchuria.	滿州
Denmark.	丁抹	Manila.	馬尼拉
England.	英國,英吉利	Mediterranean Sea, (Chichūkai).	地中海
Egypt.	埃及	Mexico.	墨西哥
Europe.	歐羅巴	Moukden.	盛京
Formosa, (Taiwan).	臺灣	Nankin.	南京
France.	佛國,佛蘭西	Newchang.	牛莊

New York.	紐	育	Siberia.	西比利亞	
Norway.	諾	威	Singapore.	新嘉坡	
Paris.	巴	里	Sŏul, (Keijō).	京 城	
Pacific Ocean, (Taiheiyō).	太平洋		Spain.	西班牙	
Pekin.	北	京	Sweden.	瑞 典	
Persia.	波	斯	Switzerland.	瑞 西	
Peru.	秘	露	Taku.	大 沽	
Philippine Islands.	比律賓諸島		Tamsui.	淡 水	
Port Arthur, (Rio-jun-kō).	旅順口		Tientsin.	天 津	
Port Hamilton, (Kio-bun-tō).	巨文島		Thursday Island.	木曜島	
Portugal,	葡萄牙		Tongking.	東 京	
Prussia.	普魯士		Turkey.	土耳其	
Red sea, (Kōkai).	紅 海		United States of America, (Beikoku, Gasshū-koku).	米國,合衆國	
Rome.	羅 馬		Vladivostok.	浦鹽斯德	
Russia.	露國,魯西亞		Washington.	華盛頓	
Saghalien, (Karafuto).	樺 太		Weihaiwei, (I-kai-ei).	威海衛	
Saigon.	柴 根		Yangtse River, (Yōsukō).	楊子江	
San Francisco.	桑 港		Yellow Sea, (Kwōkai).	黄 海	
Shanghai.	上 海		Yuensan, (Gen-zan).	元山津	
Siam.	暹 羅				

ERRATA.

On page 2, second line, the ON of the 35th Radical should be " Jo, NIO," not " Jō, NIŌ."
,, ,, 15, first ,, under the character 倒, read " Taoreru" for " Taoru."
,, ,, 26, fifth ,, ,, ,, ,, 右, there should be a comma after " designation."
,, ,, 30, ,, ,, ,, ,, ,, 嚇, read " odosu" for " odoru."
,, ,, 33, last ,, ,, ,, ,, 電, ,, " p*l*ace " ,, " p*i*ace."
,, ,, 40, first ,, ,, ,, ,, 寅, ,, " twe*l*ve " ,, " twe*i*ve."
,, ,, 41, ,, ,, ,, ,, ,, 將, add the KUN " hikiyuru."
,, ,, 57, fifth ,, ,, ,, ,, 搖. read " scoop" for " scoup."
,, ,, 62, last ,. ,, ,, ,, 敲, ,, " knoc*k* ",, " knoc*h*."
,, ,, 63, third ,, ,, ,, ,, 斜, ,, " containing " for " contaiñing."
,, ,, 73, last ,, ,, ,, ,, 段, there should be a comma after " platform."
,, ,, 75, third ,, ,, ,, 決, ,, ,, ,, ,, ,, ,, " properly."
,, ,, 85, last ,, ,, ,, ,, 栂, omit the ON, " RITSU."
,, ,, 89, ,, ,, ,, ,, ,, 橿, read " kasa" for " kaga."
,, ,, 98, ,, ,, ,, ,, ,, 誓, add the word " class."
,, ,, 99, third ,, ,, ,, ,, 菌, read " toads*t*ool" for " toadstood."
,, ,, 101, fourth ,, ,, ,, ,, 紀. ,, " chronic*l*e" ,, " chronic*al*."
,, ,, 108, first ,, ,, ,, ,, 肱. ,, " e*l*bow" for " e*ll*ow."
,, ,, ,, second ,, ,, ,, ,, 宵, there should be a comma after " Seoul."
,, ,, 130, fifth ,, ,, ,, ,, 逆. ,, ,, ,, ,, ,, ,, " Sakau."
,, ,, 133, first ,, ,, ,, ,, 那. ,, ,, ,, no ,, " complimentary."
,, ,, 135, fourth ,, ,, ,, ,, 勦. ,, ,, ,, n ,, after " spade."
,, ,, 138, second ,, ,, ,, Radical 又, read " Hiū" for " Hiu."
,, ,, 142, fifth ,, ,, ,, character 警, there should be a comma after " noise."
,, pages 152 and 153, for 211st, 212nd and 212rd Radical, read 211th, 212th and 213th respectively.
The 124th Radical (羽) is to be found on page 105, not on page 106; the 129th and 130th Radicals (聿 and 肉), on page 107, not on page 106; and the 148th Radical (角), on page 120, noton page 119.

www.ingramcontent.com/pod-product-compliance
Lightning Source LLC
Chambersburg PA
CBHW020305170426
43202CB00008B/507